# Unlocking
# Church Doors

BOOKS IN THE LEADERSHIP INSIGHT SERIES

*Unlocking Church Doors: Ten Keys to Positive Change*
**Paul Mundey**

*Leading Your Ministry*
**Alan E. Nelson**

*Body Building: Creating a Ministry Team Through Spiritual Gifts*
**Brian Kelley Bauknight**

*The Pastor's Start-Up Manual: Beginning a New Pastorate*
**Robert H. Ramey, Jr.**

LEADERSHIP INSIGHT SERIES
LEADERSHIP INSIGHT SERIES
LEADERSHIP INSIGHT SERIES

# Unlocking Church Doors

*Ten Keys to Positive Change*

HERB MILLER, EDITOR

*A moment of insight is worth a lifetime of experience*

## PAUL MUNDEY

*Abingdon Press*
*Nashville*

UNLOCKING CHURCH DOORS:
TEN KEYS TO POSITIVE CHANGE

*Copyright © 1997 by Abingdon Press*

*This book is printed on recycled, acid-free paper.*

**Library of Congress Cataloging-in-Publication Data**

Mundey, Paul, 1951–
    Unlocking church doors: ten keys to positive change/Paul Mundey
    Herb Miller, editor.
        p.   cm.—(Leadership insight series)
    Includes bibliographical references.
    **ISBN 0-687-03087-0** (alk. paper)
        1. Christian leadership.   2. Change (Psychology)—Religious aspects—Christianity.
    3. Church renewal.   I. Miller, Herb.
II. Title.   III. Series.
BV652. 1.M86      1996                                                              96-42569
253—dc20

Scripture quotations are taken from the New Revised Standard Version Bible, Copyright 1989 by the Division of Christian Education of the National Council of the Churches of Christ in the USA. Used by permission.

An excerpt from Arlin Rothauge, *Sizing Up the Congregation for New Member Ministry*, is reprinted by permission of the Domestic and Foreign Missionary Society of the Protestant Episcopal Church USA.

97 98 99 00 01 02 03 04 05 06—10 9 8 7 6 5 4 3 2 1

MANUFACTURED IN THE UNITED STATES OF AMERICA

*To my mother,*
*Anna Rebecca Mundey,*
*who pondered much the plight and*
*promise of congregations*

# CONTENTS

*Contents*

# FOREWORD

I s the willingness to change one of the major predictors of congregational health and vitality?

The following tabulations from Sunday-morning opinion surveys in two very different kinds of congregations seem to point in that direction:

| Congregation A | Congregation B | |
|---|---|---|
| 393 | 14 | —energetic and open to new ideas |
| 91 | 27 | —flexible on some issues, rigid on others |
| 0 | 217 | —slow moving and resistant to change |
| 0 | 43 | —standing still |
| 2 | 31 | —losing ground |
| 6 | 6 | —other (please describe) |

In Congregation A, average worship attendance has grown from 346 to 742 during the past ten years. Congregation B has been riding a downward membership spiral for two decades. Formerly three times as large, this church appears to have a date with the dinosaurs at some point in its future.

Congregation A, less than twenty years old, has just voted to relocate. It is purchasing a thirty-acre site two miles away that allows for continued membership growth. In Congregation B, the pastor is trying to convince the worship committee that a greater variety of hymn types might be spiritually meaningful to younger adult worshipers. The committee is not buying that idea. "If they don't like the kinds of hymns we sing, they can go somewhere else," the chairperson said. (Unfortunately, many young adult members and worship visitors have already done that.)

Willingness to change is not the only factor that makes churches effective or defective. Yet change resistance often keeps other assets—friendliness, good preaching, and a caring atmosphere—from accomplishing their mission. Congregation B possesses all three of those positive qualities, but its lack of openness to new ideas has caused hundreds of people to vote with their absence.

Change comes in two forms: individual and group. Eleanor Roosevelt is often cited as an illustration of courageous change, and she certainly deserves that pedestal. The story is told that when she became First Lady, she announced her intention of operating the White House elevator herself. Horrified, the chief usher said, "That just isn't done, Mrs. Roosevelt."

"It is now," she said, entering alone and closing the door.

Group change, however, is infinitely more complicated than solo change, especially in churches. Had Eleanor Roosevelt tried to change that elevator tradition with a group of church leaders, the process likely would have taken much longer. In churches, group habits grow into traditions bronzed with religious authority. Pragmatic procedures not originally considered sacred begin to take on moral value in the minds of their users. Over time, convenient optional practices become concreted into "the way we've always done it."

Paul Mundey makes a unique contribution to this complex church leadership issue. Many books illustrate the need for change in congregations. This one provides practical suggestions for accomplishing that art/science. Many books address change theory. This one provides a toolbox of ideas that work among frontline practitioners who are trying to transform B congregations into A congregations.

A leader is, by definition, a change agent. (Leaders who bring about no changes are followers rather than leaders.) A leader has the courage to say, "Let's do this differently!" and the skill to help people migrate from present to future while enjoying the trip. A leader knows (a) what to change; (b) how to change it; (c) when to change it; and (d) who to enlist in persuading others to move in a new direction. Mundey provides insights for accomplishing those crucial activities.

Every human group wants progress. Yet a majority of group members block that progress because, unconsciously, they are addicted to defective thinking habits. What they really want is progress without change. Since this rarely happens, a leader must help people break that addiction and become comfortable with the idea of progress *with* change. Mundey tells leaders how to do that.

Herb Miller,
Lubbock, Texas

# INTRODUCTION

Scientist Jean-Henri Fabre once conducted an experiment with processionary caterpillars. After enticing a group of larvae out of their natural habitat, Fabre placed them on the rim of a large flowerpot. After he arranged the caterpillars in their usual posture, each with its head fitted snugly against the rear extremity of the next, they began moving around and around. The naturalist expected that they would soon tire of their methodical pace. Not so. Through force of habit, the living, creeping circle kept its accustomed pattern for seven days and nights. Only exhaustion and starvation interrupted the larvae's relentless routine.

Fabre had placed an ample supply of food just inches from the flowerpot. But the caterpillars were required to leave their familiar circle to eat it. Stuck in the same old routine, bound by the beaten path, they chose not to reach for an obvious source of life.

Unfortunately, caterpillars aren't the only ones bound by the beaten path. Countless congregations are as well. Instead of advancing the cause of Christ, scores of local churches wander in endless circles, mistaking activity for accomplishment. Such congregations desire new levels of nourishment and vitality, but they resist breaking the circle of their routine. Progress without adjustment, maturation without modification, is their common expectation.

# A Different Desire

The Scriptures, however, reveal a different desire for churches. Again and again, we see evidence that God yearns for his people to move beyond unproductive old patterns into effective, new ways of life. Throughout the Bible we find God uplifting the theme of advancement through transformation and life-change (Isa. 43:18-10; Ezek. 11:14-21; 2 Cor. 5:16-21; Eph. 4:17-32). Following the same pattern of life relentlessly is not God's intention for us. Rather, repentance, conversion, and new creation is God's design and expectation. Though seasons of stability and sameness are part of the Creator's pattern, they are best viewed as periods of incubation, during which new expressions of transformational life wait to be born.

Leadership is the primary catalyst for bringing God's transformation to congregations. Churches will not change without the initiative and courage of skilled people pointing the way. John Kotter of the Harvard Business School observes:

> The most common function of effective leadership in modern complex organizations [is] to produce change, often dramatic change, in some useful direction. . . . Indeed, the promise of major change for the better is at the very heart of what leadership is all about. It always has been.[1]

Such a mandate, however, does not require a superhuman figure remaking subordinates into miracle workers. Rather, it assumes a process that, in the words of John Kotter, involves hundreds, even thousands of "little acts of leadership."[2] This volume unlocks ten principles to facilitate such a style of positive leader initiative. As you work through this book, you will discover how to:

1. model life-change, leading from your own experience;
2. cast a vision for what can be;
3. connect with the culture of your people;
4. understand your congregation as a complex system of systems;
5. create opportunities for persons to learn, grow, and change;
6. name needs, inviting others to help define solutions;
7. be alert to the reality of transition;
8. launch changes well;
9. reduce, rather than resist resistance;
10. take steps to solidify your new beginning.

The ten chapters that illustrate these principles do not favor a particular bias for implementation. You can incorporate these principles in your church through a systematic process (long-range planning committee; yearly goals and budget retreat; intervention by a professional consultant) or by a simple process, focusing on one or more immediate ministry needs. The material focuses on equipping pastors, though administrative board members and other lay leaders will find applications for their work as well.

These chapters draw on original research gleaned from the Change and the Established Congregation Project. Details about the research and participants may be found in the appendix.

## Beyond Locked Doors

Socially acceptable insanity can be defined as "doing the same things in the same way, but expecting different results." Such experience marks much of our behavior pattern, especially in churches. Jesus challenges us, however, to move beyond stubborn habits and barriers toward new discovery.

On Easter evening, Jesus' disciples gathered in a Jerusalem hiding place, fearful of the Jewish authorities. The Gospel writer John tells us that they huddled behind "locked" doors. But then Jesus appeared in their midst, moving beyond the secure, bolted entrance. And Jesus said, "Peace be with you" (John 20:19).

This scriptural picture challenges us to move with Christ beyond the fastened doors and obstinate obstacles blocking positive congregational change, toward new life and shalom. The ten chapters that follow provide practical tools for transformation as we journey on with Jesus.

# CHAPTER 1

# THE NEWNESS OF YOU

## PRINCIPLE: MODEL LIFE-CHANGE, LEADING FROM YOUR OWN EXPERIENCE

I'd have to say the heart attack is the best thing that ever happened to me."

So confesses Charles Simpson, an assertive, achievement-focused pastor from upstate New York. After years of attempting to "bring in the Kingdom" through his own zeal, a coronary emergency brought him to a screeching but revealing halt.

In the months that followed his attack, Simpson radically restructured his routine. He changed his diet; he changed his exercise routine; he changed his spiritual life; he changed his time management.

"I did more than recover from a heart attack!" Simpson declares. "I discovered a new whole new way of living. I'm taking better care of myself emotionally, intellectually, physically, and spiritually. I'm sorry it took a major crisis to get my attention. I've always been an obsessive-compulsive type, living out of 'shoulds and oughts.' I've discovered a measure of grace now, and it's touched my life for the better. By learning some healthy self-care, my whole perspective has changed. I now look at both my family and the congregation with new eyes. What a difference!"[1]

Why do we reflect on Charles Simpson's story as we begin a book on congregational change? Self-change is not our preferred starting place as we contemplate altering the life and inner workings of a particular church. But such self-examination and transformation are essential. To paraphrase Gandhi: We must become the change we wish others to become.

## *PRINCIPLE:*
## *MODEL LIFE-CHANGE,*
## *LEADING FROM YOUR OWN EXPERIENCE*

Change flows from the "inside out." A leader's use of technology and intellect, by itself, does not bring organizational turnaround. Rather, change emerges out of a life that God has touched and transformed. Norman Shawchuck restates this truth: "When it comes to forming a congregation in the Spirit of Christ, two things of importance stand out in bold relief: First . . . the pastor cannot lead where he or she has never been. Second, the congregation will not journey beyond the pastor."[2]

# Getting the Funnel Right Side Up

A pastor was less than diligent in preparing for a particular preaching event. He had turned his attention to other demands—avoiding the rigors of solitude, study, and prayer. When Sunday morning came, he mounted the pulpit with confidence. Boldly, he announced to the congregation that more pressing ministry concerns had prevented him from writing out a sermon—but have no fear, he said, the Holy Spirit would meet him in this moment.

"When I find myself in this kind of circumstance," he explained, "I always imagine a large funnel atop my head. Into this funnel, God pours his wisdom, minute by minute, as I preach."

The pastor then preached—poorly. One man, leaning over to his wife, commented, "I think his funnel is pointing in the wrong direction!"

Personal transformation begins when a leader aligns his or her "funnel" in the right direction. Such positioning happens best through personal order, balance, and discipline. Psychologist M. Scott Peck is right: "Without discipline, we can solve nothing."[3]

Five tactics can stimulate the kinds of personal discipline that lead to positive change: (1) postpone pleasure; (2) behave your beliefs; (3) manage time; (4) care for yourself; and (5) foster attitudes of expectancy.

### *Postpone Pleasure*

This discipline involves a willingness to delay enjoyment in order to participate in more demanding, but growth-oriented aspects of life—for example, reading the scholarly journal before switching on the evening news, or making the difficult phone call before jumping in the pool.

The key to mastering this discipline is advance decision making. In order to successfully delay pleasure, we must decide our priorities before we meet our experiences.

Wally Lawson struggled with weight loss for many years; his particular weakness was Ben and Jerry's ice cream. Try as he might, he could not resist diving into a pint of Rain Forest Crunch every time he opened the refrigerator freezer. Through counseling with a friend, he discovered that his real moment of reckoning was not in front of the refrigerator freezer, but rather in front of the grocery store freezer. Wally made the decision to indulge in Ben and Jerry's well before any compulsive cravings in the kitchen. We manage impulses as we strategize in advance how to head off undisciplined cravings.

What impulses do you need to head off through advance decision making? Where do you need to postpone pleasure in order to achieve a greater sense of progress and fullness?

### Behave Your Beliefs

Unless we set boundaries, life runs by impulsive whim. Beliefs and values help to define the parameters, moving us through a routine with order, decency, and hope—avoiding side roads. "Practice without belief is a forlorn existence. Managers [leaders] who have no beliefs but only understand methodology and quantification are modern-day eunuchs."[4]

What are the values that define a Christian's lifestyle? Integrity, humility, fidelity, temperance, courage, justice, patience, industry, simplicity, and modesty, to name a few. Rooting ourselves in these kinds of values provides fertile ground for positive change—rather than reckless change.

A few years ago, a recounting of basic virtues to church leaders would have seemed redundant. In 1985, for example, 67 percent of those interviewed by the Gallup Poll rated the honesty and ethics of clergy as very high or high. As a result of the increase of sexual and fiscal misconduct among clergy, however, that figure is declining, down to only 54 percent in 1992. Given the slippage in clergy respect and ethics, we must underscore even rudimentary principles of morality. We do not institute change or succeed at any cost. We must behave our beliefs, working within moral and ethical boundaries.

## *Manage Time*

We often "kill" time, but we seldom *manage* it. Like a disorganized desk, a disorganized calendar serves as a catalyst to stir up chaos in our lives. Yet with a few simple steps, you can perform CPR on personal time management.

*1. Quantify your day.* Time seems to slip away because we do not think of it as a perceptible, tangible resource. Visualize your day as 24 hours, 1440 minutes, and 86,400 seconds. No day will have more units of time, or less. It is your decision as to how you use or squander this precious commodity.

*2. Keep a "to do" list.* This simple organizational tool is a basic for time management.
- Write the list out by hand, or print it on your computer—every day.
- Prioritize items on your daily sheet, 1 through 5.
- Motivate yourself by crossing off completed items with a large marker in bold fashion.

*3. Think monthly.* In addition to any weekly listing of events, keep a big and prominent calendar of your monthly schedule. Keeping your life visual over a 28- to 31-day period is a wonderful way to keep a big-picture view of your routine. When your commitments are clearly in view, they become more manageable and within your control.

*4. Divide and conquer.* Break complex projects into manageable segments. This strategy is not applicable only to military campaigns; it can help you regain sanity in your schedule.

For example, rather than rushing to complete the church newsletter article in a single day, block out three time periods on three separate days. During one time interval, generate ideas, letting your thought process flow. During a second time period, write out your basic thoughts in a first draft. During a third time interval, rework your ideas, writing a finished draft.

*5. Consolidate movement.* Do not respond to each phone call as it is received; rather, return all calls during a single time block. Combine errands: when you are out shopping, also get your hair cut and drop off your dry cleaning. Cluster your responsibilities.

Effective time management creates space not only to accomplish our ministry, but also to assess our ministry. As a general rule of thumb, we should set aside 80 percent of our time for current assignments, but reserve 20 percent for review, reflection, and evaluation.

Leaders lose sight of the next step on the journey without blocks of time to ask probing, searching questions: Where am I? Where are we as a congregation? Where do I/we need to regroup, pull back, or move ahead?

## Care for Yourself

A cartoon pictured a disheveled wreck of a man riding on a bus. Striking up a conversation, a woman inquired whether the man was ill.

"No," he replied, "I'm in the ministry."

Out of shape church leaders cast doubt on the discipline of their lives and also on the possibilities for real change. Though servanthood is at the heart of the Christian vocation, it must never push aside the necessity of regular exercise, balanced eating, and recreation. Evidence of personal well-being speaks volumes on the probability of corporate well-being.

Church consultant Roy Oswald explains that "Self care cannot be a peripheral issue for clergy. The Medium is the Message. Anything we can do to increase our health, physically, emotionally . . . proportionally increases our effectiveness as a religious authority. Only 30% of communication is verbal; 70% is non-verbal. Health and wholeness communicates powerfully."[5]

Depending on our season of life, each of us will approach self care in distinct ways. Some will embark on a program of vigorous conditioning at the local fitness center. Others will simply watch more carefully fat, sodium, or calorie intake. Still others will seek out a mental-health professional to work on issues of midlife or family of origin. The particular route of wholeness is not important; what is important is to pursue some avenue toward greater health and personal vigor.

## Foster Expectant Attitudes

Psychiatrist Viktor Frankl spent several brutal years in a Nazi concentration camp. While incarcerated in that setting, Frankl clarified much of

21

life, including the ultimate determinants of survival. He concluded that of the three basic realities of life—the experiential (reality beyond our control), the creative (reality we initiate), and the attitudinal (our response to reality)—the attitudinal is the most potent.[6]

The attitude we adopt literally shapes us. What happens to us neither helps or harms us; it is our response to a particular incident that helps or harms us. What we expect is often what we get. An outlook that is hopeful, positive, proactive, and spirited often generates such outcomes; an outlook that is pessimistic, bleak, and cynical often generates those outcomes. The mind is a powerful change agent, shaping events in expectant or foreboding ways.

# Soulwork

Personal change is unlikely without discipline, but discipline is nearly impossible without soulwork. Cultivating the spiritual side of life pumps energy into discipline, empowering leaders to postpone pleasure, behave their beliefs, manage their time, care for themselves, and keep expectant.

In reflecting on the renewal of her life and ministry, United Methodist Pastor Martha Matteson underscores the work of the Holy Spirit and spiritual development: "I can't stress that enough. . . . We don't go into these things being our own change agent. . . . We go into them as weak, frail, fragile, human beings, and that only as we allow God to use us does . . . change take place."[7]

No easy, "pat" formula exists for achieving spiritual strength. Three general principles, however, provide a pathway for the leader as he or she embarks on soulwork.

## Get Away

Many of us experience spiritual dryness because too many people have too much access to our lives. Wise change agents learn to retreat periodically to safe places—places where only God and the stirrings of our spirit have access.

Fortunately, we do not need to wait until we can visit a formal retreat center to experience a "safe place." If we are observant, we can discover possibilities for refuge all around us: an isolated reading corner in a nearby public library; a well-worn easy chair in a home study; a familiar booth at a coffee shop during "off" hours; a car, either parked or traveling along a calming stretch of road; a cabin located in a special pocket of God's creation.

## Slow Down

Getting away, whatever its pattern and style, beckons us to slow down. Spiritual growth germinates as we cease striving in our lives, pausing for God's words and God's warnings.

Former judicatory executive Earl Ziegler tells of heading down a familiar Pennsylvania road. He came to a large barricade with a sign "Road Closed." Certain that he knew the highways and byways of Lancaster County better than any construction crew, Earl barreled on through. But he discovered that the road indeed came to a dead end. As he headed back the way he came, he noticed a sign scrawled on the reverse side of the dead-end barricade: "We told you it was closed."

We do not gain directional insights as we barrel through the barricades of life—as we continue to strive, strive, strive. People who want to bring about change must learn to slow down and listen to the language of silence. Practical methods for cultivating stillness include: keep a journal; write out your prayers; use a devotional book; set aside a regular Sabbath day; use reflection exercises and guided meditation. Different methods work for different people, but all serve a similar purpose—they give us a new sense of bearing, emerging only as we slow down, read the signs, and connect with God's wisdom and warning.

## Band Together

Along with the introspection that comes with getting away and slowing down, we need the empowerment of banding together, of finding soulmates on the journey of life and ministry.

For more than a decade, Dick Shreckhise, pastor of the Annville Church of the Brethren, has included an intentional spiritual friendship in his relational world. For him, such affiliation is a key source of accountability, important enough to make time for, usually on a weekly basis:

"It is a confessional time, it is a time when you can just hear from another person the forgiveness and grace of God spoken, and so it moves into those kinds of depths of confession and tears and struggle. We also rejoice with one another, and we ask of each other, 'How is the spiritual discipline in your life going?' It has just been a wonderful, wonderful discipline."[8]

Soulmates point out and explain the things of God, opening up new worlds. In seeking spiritual companionship, pray a prayer like this: "God, lead into my life people who can help me grow toward you." As you pray, be alert to those God leads in your direction. Also, take initiative yourself. Ask friends and colleagues about their interest in prayer partnerships or other forms of spiritual friendship. Inquire whether covenant groups or support groups in your area are open to newcomers. Be expectant.

## Expanding Our Minds

Discipline, undergirded by rigorous soulwork, conditions leaders to tackle the world around them. It also equips leaders to grapple with the world coming toward them. Albert Einstein once mused, "The significant problems we face cannot be solved at the same level of thinking we were at when we created them."[9] Expanded thinking, then, is necessary as we face the future.

Church leaders must expand their own thinking as a first step in expanding the thinking of congregations. Enlarging our perspective pushes the throttle of personal growth. It challenges us to rearrange our understanding, moving us beyond conventional wisdom and the status quo.

Lutheran pastor John Carlson was disturbed by conventional thinking regarding senior proms in his Minnesota community. These events were clearly designed primarily for the popular and the beautiful; the less-than-gorgeous and unathletic were conspicuously left out.

And so Carlson designed a dance event for those not normally included. He called it the "Reject Prom." It was expressly for those who did not have dates and was held the same night as the regular senior prom. It materialized into an outstanding event, full of excitement, color, and pizzazz.

In subsequent years, word got out about the popularity of the Reject Prom. The Timex Corporation, along with other companies, donated gifts to each person attending. Newspapers and other media covered the prom and gave it positive coverage. Before long, the Reject Prom began competing with the regular prom, drawing attendees from that event to the "party for losers."[10]

Such is the power of a stretched mind, a thought process reaching for the future. Rejects are embraced, as new notions of the kingdom of God break forth. Consider the following suggestions for stretching our minds:

## Recognize Paradigms

Paradigms are the lenses or containers that define, shape, and structure our thinking. New thinking evolves as we liberate our thought patterns from old confines (paradigms) and view old problems through new forms and environments. Such a process is what futurist Joel Barker calls "strategic exploration"—the investigation of new coalitions, new forms, and new methods. For example, a particular set of instruments and music often defines our church thinking with regard to worship. A paradigm shift in this area involves moving beyond this thought process and exploring new instruments and patterns.

Christ United Methodist Church in Memphis, Tennessee, has moved in this direction. The church holds a weekly service called "Saturday Night Alive," featuring "The Lord's Most Dangerous Band." Praise singers lead the worship with joyful upbeat music. The liturgy is contemporary, the dress casual.

The paradigm shift needed in one congregation, however, is often different from the shift needed in another locale. Prayerfully examine the forms and traditions that define parts of your church's ministry. Is the intent of a particular program or event stifled by an outdated way of doing things? Where might a new "container" or delivery vehicle for God's work be necessary?[11]

## Be Aware of Future Trends

As the twenty-first century nears, research abounds on future trends. When we are aware of these developments, our thinking is not only new but contextual. In the *Easum Report,* a Net Results newsletter feature focusing on forces transforming ministry in the twenty-first century, William Easum lists a number of observations that alter—profoundly—future ministry thinking. What do the following trends mean to your congregation?

1. The vast majority of the population born after 1961 have never been inside a church. The questions brought to worship will be different than they were in the past.

25

2. Cultural diversity is resulting in tension throughout North America. Affinity groups will become more important.
3. Membership in established churches is so old that it is impossible for denominational membership to increase over the next 25 years.
4. Most population growth will be from immigration.
5. The population of North America continues to age. The results are a growing need for elder care, a tremendous loss of present income, and "baby boomers" turning 50.[12]

If the church exists for the world, not for itself, the Christian community must maintain keen awareness of its mission field. Keeping track of future trends helps us be in touch with the arena of our outreach with sensitivity and competence.[13]

## Engage in Continuing Education

In reviewing keys to the vitality of her leadership, Pennsylvania pastor Margaret Twesme accents the importance of ongoing learning:

> Well for me . . . one of the things that I just think is so vital . . . is for the pastor and the leadership to be feeding themselves continuing education. . . . That is something that I have to admit I've been very conscious of, whether it is taking courses in areas that I am not familiar with such as evangelism and church growth [or] taking continuing education classes on preaching and on biblical studies.[14]

Continuing education can take many forms other than course work and graduate study. Books and newsletters can stimulate new and provocative ideas.[15] Travel engages all five learning faculties (senses) and alters one's entire frame of reference. Workshops and seminars are available within easy driving time of most parishes.[16] Extended leaves and sabbaticals are other attractive options.

In whatever way, continue to grow and learn, saturating your mind with new discovery.[17]

## Risk Entering New Networks

Most of us huddle with authors and periodicals of one particular theological persuasion, avoiding thinkers in other scholarly habitats. Established church leaders often take their cues from periodicals such as *The Christian Century* or *The Christian Ministry*. Evangelical leaders generally look to periodicals such as *Christianity Today* or *Leadership Journal* for resourcing and counsel. When we venture into other theological "camps," however, we can glean whatever creativity or wisdom is found there. Such a sojourn does not mean defection from one's own tradition or intellectual integrity. Rather, it is an admission that God's insight is seldom restricted to a particular tradition or denominational praxis.

## Get Real

Expanded thinking and the change strategies of spiritual growth and self-discipline are not enough. We need another component: weakness. An essential element in the willingness to change is the ability to be vulnerable.

A pastors' conference headlined an unusual theme: "Getting Real." Such a title suggests the need to break linkages between perfection and transformation—such as the compulsive need to speak only of spiritual victories, not of spiritual struggles. The Scriptures teach that God is changing us into the likeness of Christ. It is false witness, then, to act as if we already have arrived. Confessing the need for continuing growth is an honest and powerful sign of Christian maturation.

Vulnerable living is a powerful but painful route to transformation. It continually leads us into risky territory. But risk we must. Strategies for becoming more vulnerable and transparent as a leader are, of course, a matter of individual choice. For Jim Chronister, pastor of a growing midsized church in New Paris, Ohio, it meant coming to terms with burnout:

"What I saw happening to me was that slowly but surely, I had begun taking responsibility for the church, and I actually was not living my vision of empowering folks; I was disempowering folks," he admits. "I was trying to control things. . . . I just knew I was burned out and I was assuming too much responsibility."[18]

And so Chronister confessed his condition to his lay leadership and negotiated intentional time off. His vulnerability was a turning point in his ministry and in the vitality of his congregation.

"When I came off my sabbatical," he recalls, "I made a personal commitment to myself that first and foremost, I am responsible for my own spiritual life, that leadership for me is not a matter of creating programs that make the church grow. Leadership is really being intentional on your own personal walk, and leading a life that is a real example. So I am committed to the fact that my first calling here at the church is to work on my spiritual life and to walk closer to God. Secondly, my calling is to empower the other leaders, and I am recommitted to that."[19]

How can you demonstrate a pilgrimage of both achievement and struggle? What aspects of your own Christian growth, in process, can you share to give people a point of reference—and impetus—for their own personal development?

## Fashioned into Newness

A life of discipline, spiritual reality, expanded thinking, and personal vulnerability fashions a leader into a different kind of person. Such an individual is a man or woman with these characteristics:

### *Competence*

Leaders committed to self-change become competent leaders. An Illinois judicatory executive divides his pastors into two categories: those who are growing personally and those who are not. Growing pastors are sought after because their skill-bank is honed and expanding; passive, lethargic pastors are overlooked, viewed as incapable and out of touch.

### *Confidence*

Leaders committed to self-change also become confident leaders. Personal mastery and growth puts a bounce into your step; you lead with poise and certainty. Such a sense of self is critical; as motivational speaker John Maxwell has noted, "People follow a convictional leader, not a confused one."[20]

### *Credibility*

Leaders committed to self-change become credible leaders—believable, plausible individuals, pointing the way. Such persons have a sense of centeredness in their lives, an inner order. They relate to their congregations from the bearing of an inner compass. They can handle their parishes because they have learned to handle themselves.

Credibility is the highest compliment paid to leaders. It is a sure sign that the promise of change is present, within both the leader and the organization he or she serves.

## Pace of the Leader, Pace of the Team

The art of leadership is marked by numerous maxims, one of which is "Pace of the leader, pace of the team." A group can go no further than its leadership. If the leaders of a particular congregation are not growing and changing, chances are that the church will not grow and change either.

When leadership demonstrates personal transformation, that change creates a positive ripple effect. As leaders—clergy and laity alike—model a growing life, they affect other people—first in their immediate relationships, then throughout the congregation, and eventually into the larger community. Soon the word is out: "If life-change is what you're after, then _____ Church is the place to be."

Everyone in leadership needs to grapple with speaker John Ortberg's question, "Are we living the life we are inviting others to live?"[21] Modeling life-change is a requisite for leadership effectiveness. When a leader is changing, he or she inevitably changes others in the vicinity. What's new with you leads to something new in others.

# CHAPTER 2

# LIGHTING THE WAY

## PRINCIPLE:
## CAST A VISION FOR WHAT CAN BE

James Rouse envisioned what others could not imagine. In the late sixties, most people saw only empty fields in middle Maryland; Rouse saw a futuristic city of bustling, people-friendly communities. The result? Columbia, Maryland, a model of contemporary urban planning.

In the late seventies, most people saw only dilapidated buildings in inner-city Boston; Rouse saw a thriving metropolitan marketplace. The result? Fanquiel Hall, a model of center-city urban renewal.

In the late eighties, most people saw only ghetto blight in Northwest Washington; Rouse saw a rejuvenated, humanized community. The result? Jubilee Housing, a model of urban neighborhood revitalization, in partnership with Church of the Savior.

Change is linked to vision. Not all vision leads to change, but change seldom precedes vision. Before transformation can come to a particular situation, leaders must "see" the transformation in their own mind and heart.

## PRINCIPLE:
## CAST A VISION FOR WHAT CAN BE

Formally defined, vision is a word picture that articulates an attractive, magnetic future for an organization; it is the bright beacon that pulls and

30

inspires toward a desirable tomorrow. A vision does not call for change for the sake of change; rather, it views the altering of congregational status quo as a way to achieve a healthier, more faithful expression of life in Jesus Christ.

## The Leader Is Key

A willingness to focus on vision, then, is a crucial part of leadership. As Church of the Brethren pastor Fred Bernhard affirms, "It's my job, my role, my calling. If the pastor can't have a vision or doesn't have a vision and can't share the vision, where are they [the congregation] going to go? Somebody needs to be out front holding the banner."[1]

Years of emphasis, however, on the pastor as enabler or facilitator have conditioned some of us to wince at Bernhard's words. They can be interpreted as heavy-handed or paternalistic. Yet, strong leadership needn't be synonymous with self-serving imperialistic ways. One can raise banners and set direction, as Bernhard does, in a participatory, servant-like style. Irvin Heishman, an urban pastor in central Pennsylvania, tries to reflect this melding in his own ministry:

> [I come from a tradition that works] very carefully and closely with the congregation in helping [it] have ownership . . . and I think that is very important. But at the same time, I think they need a leader who is active and assertive. . . . That doesn't mean being dictatorial, but being clear about helping the church find direction and vision.[2]

Leaders must lead; not with malice or blind ambition, but with a genuine desire to capture and implement God's dream for a particular congregation.

## Penetrating Walls of Complacency

Discovering and uplifting God's dream is a powerful catalyst for innovation. People accept change faster when they grasp a vision of the positive results coming from change. Research resulting from the Change and the Established Congregation Project found that over 98 percent of respondents agreed that effective vision-casting advances the change process.[3]

But even the most effective, inspiring visions may encounter difficult walls of complacency. Some fellowships are contented congregations that · have learned to survive in satisfactory, albeit stubborn, ways. Lyle Schaller describes such a body of believers:

> 1. They are a closely knit group of committed supporters who derive great satisfaction from a collection of meaningful, shared experiences. 2. Their gathering place has become an important "third place" (in addition to their places of residence and work) that affirms their personal identity as human beings. 3. The organization affirms and supports some deeply held cultural values that are threatened by the changing world in which they now live.[4]

Not everything about a visionless congregation is negative; in reality, such churches serve a meaningful purpose for many people in the present tense. They simply lack direction and the probability of a viable future tense.

## Vision Marks

The pioneers who blazed a trail into the wilderness watched for milestones or markers to guide the way; so too should we, as we blaze a trail into tomorrow. What are the marks of an effective vision path? At least three are prominent:

### *Visions Are Uplifting*

Visions motivate people to dream again. When vision is up and running, people feel that the best is yet to be. They believe again, they hope again. They sense that a cause bigger than their own concerns rises up before them, worthy of time, commitment, and money.

Evelyn United Methodist Church was a small, struggling, southern congregation. Through discernment and prayer, the members caught a new vision for reaching unchurched children—even though their nursery and Sunday school programs were defunct. By going door to door, they invited children to their church. They began to send vans and buses into the community to accommodate children who needed transportation.

Before long, a formal program evolved, which they named Wacky Wednesday. United Methodist consultant Joe Harding picks up the story:

> They began to have so many children that they had to have more adults helping them, so as more adults got involved, the enthusiasm and energy began to grow, and these adults were trained, not only to minister to these children . . . but also to share their faith. There were conversions of the children and their families . . . and the whole church has been radically changed from draining/tired/negative to enthusiastic/positive/upbeat.[5]

Visions lift people, propelling them toward growth, vitality, and renewal.

## Visions Set a Direction

Over the years, we have seen a recurring confusion over the difference between mission statements and vision statements. Though one could argue that the terms are interchangeable, for our purposes we will make this distinction: a mission statement states the purpose of your congregation; a vision statement states the direction of your congregation. Both are important and both serve defining roles. Burt Nanus illustrates from the world of agriculture:

> A vision is not a mission. . . . For example, the mission of a farmer hasn't changed in thousands of years: it is to grow food and bring it to market at a price that pays for all the costs of production and provides an acceptable standard of living (or profit) for the farmer. However, one particular farmer might have a vision for passing on to his children a farm with twice the acreage he currently has, while another may dream about opening a canning operation on her property, and a third may aim to be a pioneer in growing organic vegetables.[6]

The basic mission or purpose of the church hasn't changed in thousands of years. It is shared by every congregation. What does vary, however, is the application of that mission from local church to local church. Applying the mission of the church to your local context is an exciting adventure, resulting in new direction, unique callings, and fresh vision for tomorrow.

## *Visions Are Future-Oriented, But Build on the Past*

A visionary does not reject all that has been. The wise vision caster creates a launching pad out of yesterday, as a means of propelling an organization or group into tomorrow.

One of the great renewal stories is of the restoration of Baltimore's inner harbor. Once the site of dilapidated warehouses and polluted water, it is now a premier tourist attraction. How did this happen? In developing this area, civic leaders followed a key principle: reveal and incorporate the old while bringing in the new.

Consider the row houses that ring the southern end of the harbor. Once a prime target for demolition, these homes blossomed into prime real estate, in part because workers revealed their original structure and form. Patiently, they removed years of paint and layers of formstone, disclosing patterned brickwork and thoughtful craftsmanship. The workers added rooftop decks and rearranged interiors, but the motive behind these efforts was the enhancement of the original form and foundation of the building.

So, too, with our visions for change. They build on concepts, forms, and foundational principles from the past. As one German philosopher observed, "Whoever supplies memory, shapes concepts, and interprets the past will win the future."[7]

# "Voices" from God

Visions, however, are more than inspiring, clear, future-oriented, past-honoring pictures of tomorrow. Ultimately, for Christ followers, they are images of the heart and will of God. In describing her process of vision formation, Disciples of Christ pastor Kathleen Kline Chesson stresses the role of the spirit:

> The first thing I did was spend a lot of time with them [church leadership] in prayer and opening ourselves to whatever changes came. . . . Change is very frightening. You have got to function from a spiritual context. I tend to be a type-A personality, real high energy . . . but that doesn't work if I am not showing myself to be motivated by my prayer life, and I am not always good at it. I have to really struggle for that.[8]

When we as leaders prayerfully envision a future for our congregations, more is happening in our psyches than mental insight and emotional response. The very Spirit of God is at work, planting new ideas and sowing new thoughts. The imaginings of our minds become infused with the imaginings of Christ.

In George Bernard Shaw's play *Saint Joan,* Joan of Arc and Robert de Beaudricourt have the following conversation:

**Joan:** You must not talk about my voices.
**Robert:** How do you mean, voices?
**Joan:** I hear voices telling me what to do. They come from God.
**Robert:** They come from your imagination!
**Joan:** Of course. That's how the messages of God come to us.[9]

What hopes and dreams rumble through the imaginations of your congregation? What might God be saying to you about a new future for your church? Does that vision come from God? Yes! Does that vision come from your imagination? Yes! Imagination is how God transmits change-producing visions.

## Entering Our Imaginations

We capture God's vision for tomorrow by more fully tapping our creativity. Assuming, with Joan of Arc, that God is with us in our imagination, this sometimes means letting go of conscious effort, allowing our minds to roam in an attitude of prayer.

Each of us has settings and routines that trigger a free release of creative power. One church executive recounts that the best administrative decision of his career came to mind while he was in the shower. A pastor once commented that his most productive sermon ideas occur while he is cutting the lawn or engaging in some other form of physical activity. What is it for you? What fires your soul and frees your creative juices?

Once those juices are flowing, we can make the most of our imaginative energy in a number of ways.

## Doodle

Roam with your creative ideas on paper. Jot down ideas and possibilities. Draw pictures and diagrams. Turn your dream in one direction, and then the next. If you are comfortable using a computer, doodle using more advanced technology. In some way, begin to shape, form, and visualize your dreams.

## Dream

Play out various ideas in your mind. Let thoughts and feelings expand. Ask a series of "what if" questions. Picture in your mind any number of futures for your congregation. Imagine specific scenarios, with specific people, in specific places, with specific ministries.

## Dare

For the moment, think big. What would you do or suggest if you knew you couldn't fail? Don't automatically shut down various possibilities because they seem foreign, difficult, or improbable.

In sizing up his experience as an innovator at a Chicago area parish, Pastor Mark Miller-McLemore emphasizes the importance of openness:

> One of the things that has been most helpful to me as a minister and agent of change is really to be open to the possible, and not to shut down any possibility, so that there is always a silk purse to be made from a sow's ear, no matter what. There seems to be an up side to every down side. There are all sorts of remarkable things that have taken place when we have sort of said, "Let's wait and see what we can do with this, rather than throwing up our hands in despair."[10]

# Editing the Possibilities

One of the realities of our television age is the brevity of broadcast moments. For every three minutes of video televised on the evening news, sixty minutes of unused material falls on the cutting floor. The role of editor is a powerful position, influencing and shaping the outlook of many.

The leader assumes a similar role as he or she shapes a new tomorrow for congregational life. Choosing from original ideas and the promptings of God, the vision leader selects and edits possibilities, choosing those ideas that hold highest potential for a worthwhile future.

## Feel the Fit

As you edit the possibilities, how do they feel? Do your hopes and dreams mesh with your sense of self, and that of your congregation?

For years, a man complained of dizzy spells. In desperation, he tried every remedy, but nothing helped. Finally, he lost hope and began to plan his funeral. Going to a haberdasher, he picked out a new suit, especially for his burial. As he did, he asked for his standard shirt size—15. The store clerk suggested a size 16. After all, he had measured the man's neck. The ill gentleman became very indignant, insisting that he be given what he asked for—a size 15.

Finally, in exasperation, the clerk blurted out, "But sir, if you wear a size 15, you'll get dizzy spells."[11]

If some of our visions make us dizzy, it may be that they don't fit. They may not be congruent with our basic makeup as leaders or congregations. An effective idea for change must authentically link God's vision, our personality, and the identity of a particular local church. If a vision doesn't fit, it may be a delusion of grandeur, rather than God's dream and design for our particular situation.

## Focus on Your Critical Advantage

Ask a tough but strategic question: Why would an individual or family come to our congregation, rather than to a neighboring congregation? Build your vision around the critical advantage your congregation does or can offer to others.

A declining inner-city congregation in Fort Wayne, Indiana, struggled to find its critical advantage. It soon dawned on it that no congregation in that ministry area was reaching out to street people. And so the members added a worship service targeted to these folks, along with young adults. The service was at 8:00 A.M. and featured contemporary music and a relaxed format. Soon new people were drawn to the congregation, attracted by the unique, original approach of a visionary church.[12]

## Incorporate a Challenge

Persons want to be inspired and stretched as they look toward tomorow. Venture beyond the known and seen.

In rallying his Milbank, South Dakota, congregation toward completing an $800,000 building addition, Pastor Dick Boyd challenged the leadership to conduct a stewardship drive involving three-year pledges. After a year of planning, Boyd turned to the members of his building committee and said, "Now, folks, we all have to have our [pledges] in first."

As Boyd tells it, "A couple swallowed hard, but they understood. . . . I said, 'If leaders don't lead this way, you have no ground to stand on in terms of telling the congregation they should support this.' I think this helped the whole process."[13]

### Sound a Note of Realism

People want to be stretched, not broken. Visionary enterprises are not to be confused with foolhardy enterprises that shatter both dreams and people. Along with trumpet blasts of challenge and risk, people need to hear notes of measured thinking and wisdom. Surprisingly, great entrepreneurs and innovators are not high-risk people.

Rather, as Peter Drucker points out in *Innovation and Entrepreneurship*, most long-term, effective entrepreneurs exercise bounded risk. They know the probability of their success, and they structure the odds in their favor. They set up trade-offs, wherein the gains clearly outweigh the probable losses.[14] Lead your people into new territory, but avoid minefields that could explode in your face.

## Casting and Crafting

A cartoon pictured a fisherman lounging in a rowboat. His fishing pole was off to one side as he stretched out, hands behind his head. At the bow of the boat was a sign that read, "All fish welcome to jump in."

Unlike some fishing, the process of refining and crafting vision is not a stationary activity. Rather, it is an enterprise in motion, which requires the leader to cast his or her vision—untidy as it is—into a widening circle of persons.

*1.* The first ring of the circle contains people with *informal* positions of power in your congregation. These are the matriarchs and patriarchs of the congregation, the mainstays related to church life. Pitch your dream to these people with animation; then listen, listen, listen. On the basis of their input, make adjustments to your ideas and wording.

Management consultant James Belasco compares your role at this point to that of a quarterback at the line of scrimmage. You have a game plan and a specific play in mind, but you are realizing that adjustments are needed as you engage other players on the field.[15]

**2.** The second ring of the circle contains people with *formal* positions of power in the church. These are executive committee members or board members. Again, find a setting where you can share your vision; then listen, listen, listen. On the basis of their input, make further adjustments.

At this point in the process, you probably will be aware of the people who are "tracking" with you, people with whom you have a natural affinity. In partnership with your congregation's executive leadership, call together a *small* group of these people to work with you in shaping a formal vision statement. In many congregations, this group becomes a long-range planning committee or visioning committee.[16]

In shaping your statement, remember to:

*Give direction.* Remember, you are writing a *vision* statement, not a *mission* statement. Your task is to give a direction for the future. Certainly you can build upon your basic mission and purpose, but your task is to apply it in specific, selected ways for tomorrow.

*Speak simply.* Advertising executive Al Ries is right when he says, "We have become the world's first over-communicated society. Each year we send more information and receive less."[17]

*Use short sentences, vivid language, and as much specificity as possible.* Long, cumbersome concepts do not register in an age of MTV and nightly news sound bites. Using these criteria, what might a completed vision statement look like? An example follows, preceded by a sample mission statement for purposes of comparison.

**MISSION:** To continue the work of Jesus, peacefully, simply, together.

**VISION:** We want to become a community of Christ followers who demonstrate compassion for irreligious people, practice right relationships, and live out radical discipleship. Our dream is to include more young adults who live within a twenty-minute radius of our church building. While not neglecting existing members, we want to reach out to young singles and families, through relevant, effective, and faithful ministries.

This vision statement is only a sample. Yours should be unique and situational for your particular congregation. Copying another church's model can be self-defeating, since you can adopt it without going through the important process that leads to emotionally owning it.

**3.** The third and final circle of persons to influence is, of course, the entire congregation. Ultimately, the members must be the repository of any God-given vision, for without the Body of Christ, dreams fall flat, lacking form, motion, and backbone. Casting vision among the congregation occurs in two stages:

First, there is the preliminary stage that begins the first Sunday you arrive in a particular congregation. From "day one," strive to preach a steady diet of messages related to hope, promise, and the gospel's power to change human life. Pastor Ron Klassen recalls his early days in a rural parish:

> When I came, I quickly realized we needed a strong dose of encouragement. . . . From the pulpit, I told the people over and over how privileged I felt to be their pastor. . . . I preached positive sermons. . . . I wielded the power of the pen, writing hundreds of notes to members of my church.[18]

Presbyterian pastor Dennis Burnett employed other means to build anticipation and future-hope.

> Sometimes in a sermon, I will intentionally say things like "This church has a future," or I try to reorient the church's newsletter to be something that tells about what is going to happen, instead of [only] news about who served as acolytes last month. A future-focused newsletter. Hand in hand with that is just really trying to build up morale and a sense of "can do" and *esprit de corps.*[19]

The second stage of vision casting occurs as a specific congregational vision unfolds. In tandem with your preliminary work, reveal the exciting possibilities that are now becoming clear to both you and other leaders in your church. This can be done in several ways:

1. *Hold house groups.* When John R. Myers was first attempting to stir his South Bend, Indiana, congregation toward action, he held a series of "Catch the Vision" house groups. He began each meeting with a question: What is our reason for being?

"Every time I ask it," Myers recounts, "I answer it. Our reason for being is to be a magnet for God." And then he goes on to flesh out a specific vision in inspiring and captivating terms.[20]

2. *Devote a worship service to the theme of vision.* Peachtree Presbyterian Church in Atlanta, Georgia, devotes at least one Sunday a year to the theme of vision. The accent is always on new, specific challenges in the months ahead, such as the need for new social ministries, staff, or building space. Pastor Frank Harrington always includes a strong dose of inspiration, rallying his people on to greater heights:

> Let it be said that here in our city—a city of great blessings and great blight, a city of great wealth and grinding poverty, God raised up a church and called it Peachtree Presbyterian—a church that in the worst of times did the best of things. It declared that we shall press on, press on, for the mark of the high calling of God in Christ Jesus, our Lord.[21]

Refining and casting vision is a dynamic ongoing exercise. Effectively implemented, it steers the course of a congregation forward, in spite of uncertain waters and choppy seas.

## Grand Canyon Perspective

Three people were visiting the Grand Canyon—an artist, a pastor, and a cowboy. As they stood on the edge of this natural wonder, each made a heartfelt response.

The artist said, "Ah, what a beautiful scene to paint!"

The minister cried, "What a wonderful example of the handiwork of God!"

The cowboy mused, "What a terrible place to lose a cow!"[22]

Vision casting makes the big difference in the way members of a congregation view tomorrow—and the kind of tomorrow at which they arrive. A leader without vision can reduce the grandeur of God's possibilities to cow catching. A leader with vision can create a picture of God's goodness and prospects for a fruitful tomorrow that will move people rapidly toward the benefits of living there.

# CHAPTER 3

# MISSIONARY MANEUVERS

## PRINCIPLE: CONNECT WITH THE CULTURE OF YOUR PEOPLE

I magine that you have just landed in a foreign country. After moving beyond the airport, you encounter—rather quickly—new sights, sounds, and people. The fresh terrain captures your attention, but a gnawing anxiety hangs on as you struggle with foreign words and the smell of unfamiliar food. The stress only escalates as you struggle to grasp peculiar traditions, traffic patterns, and idioms. Instinctively, you check your ticket for the date of your return flight, only to discover—three more weeks to go!

Such a scene is not unfamiliar for many pastors and church leaders. Landing in a new parish or assignment, you are captivated—at first—by new people and new terrain. But then culture shock sets in as you find yourself bumping up against language, customs, beliefs, and traditions that feel foreign. Your first instinct is to flee, but with three years to go, and simply to save face, you decide to "fight." And fight you do, battling to change your predicament by changing the patterns and traditions set in your path.

Heroic? Maybe not. Alban Institute president James P. Wind contends that leaders who "have unwittingly collided with congregational cultures . . . have often perpetrated acts of violence against those cultures."[1] Granted, it is difficult to bring about change in established congregations without bringings about change in some aspect of congregational culture. However, the wise change agent neither fights nor flees, but enters into the new terrain that is part of his or her calling.

## PRINCIPLE:
## CONNECT WITH THE
## CULTURE OF YOUR PEOPLE

Such a stance does not rule out modifying congregational culture (we must if we are to bring about authentic change), it simply discourages us from beginning at that point. The secret to changing church culture is found in understanding a congregation's symbols, language, values, and stories. In this regard, the pastor/leader is much like a missionary—discovering the beauty and meaning of a foreign land.

# Symbols

Fresh from seminary, Pastor Linda Lakton attempted to bring small-group ministry to St. John's Church. After sensing the resistance of many to hold meetings in their homes, she suggested refurbishing a room in the church building for small-group use. Upon turning to the Women's Fellowship, Lakton found a project committee eager to complete the task. In the weeks that followed, she anticipated the completion of the room with great excitement. For the new pastor, it represented a place of safety, learning, and renewal—a symbol of the vision she was casting for the future.

Finally the day of completion arrived. Walking up to the room with the president of the Women's Fellowship, Pastor Lakton noticed a lock on the door. She discovered that it was there to secure the parlor. "What parlor?" she questioned. "This parlor," the Women's Fellowship President indicated, pointing to the refurbished room. As a group hailing from Appalachian heritage, the members of the Women's Fellowship had created a room designed only for weddings, funerals, and visiting ministers; for them, it represented a place of privilege and limited use—not weekly Bible studies and active learning.

What appear to be chairs to sit on and tables to place Bibles on can represent a different realm of meaning for key congregational members. Innocent looking rooms, cabinets, furniture arrangements, pictures, landscaping, and pulpit hangings can hold symbolic intentions far beyond their common use.

One new pastor asked for a young tree to be moved, since it was blocking the view out of his study. It was a fair request, from his perspective, since there was ample church acreage in need of landscaping. When he brought his idea to the Property and Finance Committee, he was met with a firestorm. Why? The tree the pastor was asking to move was the same tree planted by his predecessor only six months before, as a symbol of his ten-year ministry with that particular congregation. The new pastor saw only a tree; the Property and Finance Committee saw a beloved, former minister.

Think of your current ministry setting: What objects or settings hold symbolic power? What can be altered with sensitivity; what is clearly off limits?

## Language

Every new terrain has its own particular way of expressing words and thoughts. In new territory, you take a risk when you assume that you are automatically connecting with folks. Two good ole boys were once on the outskirts of a west Texas town. Arguing over the exact pronunciation of the metropolis, they squealed to a halt in front of the first commercial establishment in town. Running up to the counter, they implored the clerk to pronounce very slowly where they were. Obliging, the young woman replied: D A I R Y   Q U E E N.

Many leaders rush into local churches assuming that people understand our visions and needs, only to discover that these folks are on a completely different wavelength.

This was Pastor Jim Chronister's experience. Early in his ministry in rural southern Ohio, Chronister would impulsively share new program ideas with his church board—without any consideration of the ethos of his congregation. In essence, he would say, "Here's what we need to do, folks; get with the program." It is not surprising, Chronister observes, that people would react with confusion and disinterest, often never connecting with the new idea.

Now Pastor Chronister is much more selective in what he presents to the people, realizing that every new notion will not automatically fit the culture of the congregation. In addition, when he does present a new opportunity or ministry possibility, he works hard at translating it into the thought process, style, and language of his people.[2]

Historians have attempted to describe the varied languages spoken in faith communities. Some speak the language of Pentecost—a vocabulary

45

accenting the work of the Holy Spirit. Words such as "spirit-filled," "baptism with the Spirit," and "anointed" flow freely. Others speak the language of Amos—a vocabulary lifting up the prophetic. Words such as "justice," "peace," and "liberation" punctuate conversations. Still others speak the language of Calvary—a vocabulary dominated by images of the sacrifice of Christ. Words such as "born again," "washed in the blood," and "redeemed" prevail.

Beyond these languages are many more, some not as evident, but just as powerful in shaping congregational culture. The critical factor is not to place a value judgment on any of these languages, but to understand them and the deep meaning they bring to the people you seek to serve.

Seminary professor Tex Sample tells of a class in which he profiled the hymn "In the Garden." He used it to illustrate all that was wrong with popular religion: sentimentality, individualism, sloppy piety. He even "whined" a few stanzas of the hymn to drive home his point.

After class, a young woman confronted Sample: "Tex, my father started screwing me when I was eleven, and he kept it up until I was sixteen and found the strength somehow to stop it. After every one of those ordeals, I would go outside and sing that song to myself. Without that song, I don't know how I could have survived. Tex, don't you ever ever make fun of that song again!"[3]

No matter the cultural gap between your experience and those you seek to serve, never belittle language. That language communicates in your current context, and you will be wise to learn it, not for the sake of acquiescence, but for the sake of making connections—connections between where your people are and where God is calling them to be.

## Values

At the heart of understanding the culture of your congregation is understanding the values of your congregation. These values are the key beliefs or assumptions of your people. You know you have violated one or more of these unwritten understandings when you encounter the retort, "We don't do things that way around here."

Congregational values, of course, vary from place to place. In one setting, the value might be, "Debt is unbiblical; Christians pay as they go"; but in another setting, "Debt is a demonstration of faith; Christians need to risk for the future." At the outset, the legitimacy of a particular value statement is not your primary concern; what is critical is acknowledging that it is there.

As unwritten "invisible" influences, value-sets are incredibly powerful and difficult to alter. But wise pastors and lay leaders make an honest attempt. The most common mistake made by change agents is introducing a new program or ministry, without introducing a new accompanying value. Underscore this point and mark it down; it is critical to effectiveness.

Pastor Jeff Newman returned from an Evangelism Academy all fired up to help the unchurched make a life-changing connection with God. However, his congregation, Good Shepherd Church, had no experience in this form of outreach. For two decades, they had majored in ministries to the homeless and advocacy for peace and justice. Rather than introducing a new value into their belief system (affirming that unchurched people matter to God), Pastor Newman gathered together some fringe members and formed an evangelism committee. For the next six months, this group of zealots pounded away at the congregation, using the vocabulary of "shoulda, coulda, and woulda"—laying a guilt trip on the congregation. Rather than fostering the sharing of good news, this ill-founded witness effort fostered nothing but bad news.

Values are like stepping stones across a vigorous and swift stream. If we expect people to cross new currents, we first need to provide a foundation, a place for them to stand. Otherwise, the journey is too intimidating and the possibilities of being knocked off balance too likely.

What are the beliefs and assumptions of your current ministry setting? What new values need to be introduced before you institute a particular change?

## Narrative and History

A wise judicatory executive commented to a group of national staff persons, "If you want to bring about change, tie into the story, the narrative of a local church." In other words, link your new initiative to an old initiative that is revered in the tradition of your congregation.

A group of young adults in a rural northern Indiana parish caught a vision of planting a new congregation. The dream: recruit a core group of young families from the established congregation and form a new church. The initial reaction in the existing congregation was predictable: outrage

47

at the prospect of "losing a group of our young people." But a discerning lay leader intervened at a congregational business meeting, highlighting an important chapter in the story of this Indiana church.

Fifty years ago, he remarked, this mission-minded church had established a new preaching point ten miles west of town. That sacrificial move resulted in one of the strongest congregations in the district—a local church well known to all in attendance. "Our support of the new church proposed by our young adults," he went on to add, "is but a *continuation* of the history and tradition of this congregation." Though his history lesson didn't convince everyone, it mellowed the resentment brewing in the church, resulting in a positive vote for the new church project.

One of the best ways to discover the narrative of your congregation is to ask members to create a historical time line. On several sheets of newsprint taped to the wall, draw a long horizontal line. At the far right end, write the date of the current year. On the far left side, write the date of the founding of the congregation. In between, write key historical events in the life of the church, supplied by members.

As persons share, encourage them to tell stories regarding particular events. Ask them to name specific personalities, locations, even weather conditions. Invite them to enter fully into the color and texture of their history. Help participants feel the richness of their heritage and the intrinsic value of their experience. The unfolding of a congregation's story is a powerful event, identifying many connecting points and precedents for launching future ministry.

# Forces from Outside

The elements often minimized in discussions of congregational culture are the outside forces that shape a local church's symbols, language, values, and story. True, much of what forms congregational culture comes from internal factors, but external factors play a pivotal role as well. The norms of nationalism, popular culture, and mass media are three significant external elements. But there are two other major outside influences:

## *Community Influences*

A congregation cannot easily escape the impact of its geographic location. Members growing up in a particular community have been shaped by the symbols, language, values, and narrative of that community. Such influence is bound to have an effect on the symbols, language, values, and narrative of a local church. A congregation in Wiggins, Mississippi, for example, cannot easily dodge the impact of conservative, southern, rural culture, whereas a congregation in Malibu, California, cannot avoid the impact of free-spirited, West Coast, urban culture.

The impact of the geographic community is especially influential when considering the pace or rate of change within a church. As a rule of thumb, most congregations will not dramatically exceed the rate of change of their communities—especially in the early stages of renewal efforts. Consider the following newspaper account:

> When Mayor Gerard Quinn gaveled his first meeting to order at the dawn of the 1980s, Sharpsburg was a quiet residential town, with little commerce, no crime and slim opportunity for growth. Today Sharpsburg is a quiet residential town with little commerce, no crime, and slim opportunity for growth. As Quinn prepares to step down after a dozen years in office, he likes to think of it as a textbook administration.[4]

A pastor expecting rapid demonstrative tempos of change in such a community is swimming against strong cultural currents. Change in Sharpsburg, for both government and church, comes slowly and quietly. There are always exceptions to the rule, but generally, the pace or rate of change marking a church renewal initiative is influenced by the pace or rate of change marking a congregation's community context.

This is not to say that a significant change cannot occur. Recognition of environmental "rhythms" is not to be confused with environmental determinism; congregations need not be captive to their context. However, since the majority of established congregations, in the words of sociologist C. Kirk Hadaway, are "conservative, neighborhood-based organization[s] composed of entrenched social groups," energy to reverse rates of change is not easily mustered—at least initially.[5] It is probably best—especially at the outset of a change effort—to "go with the flow," stewarding one's energy toward strategies for change in keeping with the rhythm of change in a given locale.

## *Denominational Influences*

Much is written of the erosion of denominational loyalty. This is especially true in large denominational systems, far removed from the local scene. However, most congregations have been shaped in some way by the symbols, language, values, and stories of their parent body.

To illustrate: Most Presbyterian congregations have been molded by a heritage that stresses the primacy of preaching; most Mennonite congregations have been fashioned by lineage that stresses the necessity of servanthood; most Southern Baptist congregations have been formed by ancestry that stresses the centrality of biblical authority. To institute a change, then, that divorces itself from such marks of denominational culture is risky at best, destructive at worst.

This is not to suggest that congregations are to simply mimic institutionalized tradition. Respecting denominational origins is not synonymous with captivity to denominational bureaucracy. Rather, it is a call to affirm denominational vision and values, reapplying them for a new day.

Leonard Sweet has devised a three-prong formula for reaffirming and reapplying denominational heritage:

1. *Trust your tradition.* Being grounded in a rich history does not require one to be bound, restrained, and irrelevant. Roots can give way to wings. Heritage and history can inform innovation, supplying valued experience that minimizes error and the repetition of costly mistakes.

2. *Translate your tradition.* Distill your heritage into transferable concepts and values. Move beyond a denominational version of dietary laws and circumcision. What is the essence of your tradition? How can that essence be translated for people who do not share your lineage, background, or cultural language? What is applicable to a wider audience?

3. *Turbo-charge your tradition.* Make it incredibly real and pertinent. Bring it out of the historical cabinet into the churning challenges of today. Communicate your message vitally, connecting with the real needs of real people. Experiment with new forms and expressions of your heritage. Rev-up your lineage, moving it in the direction of relevancy rather than retreat.

Our summons, then, is to reinvent denominational culture, not discard it. The reinvention process can be inspiring as we contextualize denominational heritage, not only for our local setting, but for the changing paradigms of a new century.

## Connecting and Changing

We change culture by entering into it rather than fighting or fleeing. In nonmanipulative ways, we bond with the ethos of a congregation, utilizing existing symbols, language, values, and narrative to connect with future possibilities. For example, we do not discard, but incorporate the cornerstone from the old church building into the architecture of the new church building; we incorporate a powerful symbol from the past in order to construct a powerful new symbol for the future.

Becoming "one of the people" is not a professional task, but an incarnational, even earthy task. A brilliant graduate student left the University of Chicago for the back roads of Southern Alabama. His calling to ministry was clear, and a rural setting—in his mind—providential. For months he tried to relate to his people through logical arguments and rational thinking, but to no avail. Finally, he accepted a long-standing invitation to join "the boys" at the filling station. The invitation was simply to "hang out" and visit, so hang out and visit he did, even pumping gas from time to time. Reflecting, years later, on that first afternoon at the filling station, he realized that it was a turning point in his ministry. In a surprising fashion, he had bonded with a group of key leaders, creating depth, trust, and a sense of new direction.

For Pastor Jim Frisbie, bonding came not through visiting a particular place, but through adopting a new manner of dress. In pastoring the Weston United Methodist Church, he found it important to switch out of his accustomed attire of coat, tie, and wing-tips. He wore jeans. In a telephone interview, he reflected:

Here in the Pocatello area, I often would do calling on farm and ranch families in jeans and cowboy boots, and brought in some rodeo cowboys because of it. They said to me later, "You know, any preacher who comes by and visits me in jeans and cowboy boots is OK." If I had been wearing my wing-tips, I would not have been effective.[6]

What new dress pattern or routine do you need to adopt in order to bond more fully with your people? What new behavior do you need to enter into, to enter more fully into the culture and ethos of your congregation?

## The Language of Love

The business of bonding is ultimately bolstered by plain, old-fashioned loving. Jim Moss, an executive with the Churches of God, comments:

> You have to stay in touch with your people, just ahead of the people, close enough so that they can see you. . . . People will not allow you to pastor them if you don't love them. Effective pastors love their people, and you can't fool your people on that one, you just can't. You can pretend to love them, but your people will not allow you to pastor them if you don't love them.[7]

Pastor Beth Mew labored for years to advance her small membership congregation. She expanded the budget triplefold, while increasing attendance fourfold. Given her success, Beth looked forward to her five-year evaluation with much eagerness. When the night of the evaluation finally came, a few comments were made about her numerical success, but most persons commented on Beth's acts of love and kindness. The young minister was surprised.

"Pastor, I'm glad we're out of the hole budget-wise," Nona Pryor commented, "but you know what really impressed me? The fact that you took the time to ride from Lancaster, Pennsylvania, to Petersburg, West Virginia, to do my mama's graveside service. You know, you didn't have to do that, but you did."

Demonstrations of love are wide and varied: a handclasp on the shoulder of a grieving father, a note of encouragement to an anxious college freshman, an extra hand in the kitchen after the all-congregation dinner. The particular expression of caring is not the significant factor; it's simply the fact that you took the time and shared on a personal level. It's amazing how much people are willing to change when they know you care.

# On the Road to Trust

Identifying with the culture of your people, bonding with them, and loving them positions church leaders on the road to trust. Such a trajectory is important. The Change and the Established Congregation Project discovered that a majority of survey respondents believed that pastors who are trusted are in the best position to lead congregations through change.[8]

Sadly, the trust of church folk is not as easily won as in years past. Widely circulated reports of clergy misconduct and scandal have cast a shadow over the ministerial profession.

So how do you build and establish trust? In addition to the factors previously mentioned (being with folks, bonding with folks, being devoted to folks) are the following:

## Do What You Say You Are Going to Do

People trust leaders who follow through on what they promise to do. They become leery of leaders who talk a big game, but seldom deliver.

## Be Accessible and Available

People trust leaders they can reach quickly and talk to easily. On Sunday mornings, after he has finished his mental and spiritual preparation for the morning message, Texas pastor T. Mac Hood opens his office door. About this simple act, he says, "I have had numerous people say to me, 'that really impressed me. The first Sunday you were here, we saw the office door open.' Such a simple thing!"[9]

When pastors have erratic or unposted office hours, scurry away quickly after morning worship, or seem distracted during conversations, people get nervous—and untrusting.

## Admit Your Mistakes

People trust leaders who are honest about their shortcomings and foul-ups. They think twice about leaders who seem to be covering up errors and manipulating outcomes.

## Be Honest and Sincere

People trust leaders who tell the truth and speak from the heart. When pastors regularly use "waffle words" and simply parrot the party line (instead of the meditations of their own heart) people begin to have their doubts.

### *"Pay the Rent"*

People trust leaders who pay the rent before refurbishing the house.[10] They think twice about leaders who preach lousy sermons, fail to visit the sick, neglect to return phone calls, and overlook correspondence. Demonstrate competence in everyday ministerial tasks, if you want people to venture with you into the spiritual deep.

These five trust actions send a dramatic signal to waiting and watching church members: They demonstrate that you are emotionally invested in their life and future, rather than simply passing through. In the experience of American Baptist Pastor Priscilla Eppinger-Mendes, this signal is pivotal in penetrating apprehension and leeriness:

> [You have to establish] a sense of integrity and confidence, and make enough of a personal emotional investment that people don't think that you are coming in from the outside and playing games, or manipulating or changing things just for the fun of it, but have the best interest of the church at heart. That has to be the motivating force.[11]

Once established, trust becomes a launching pad onto greater heights of relationship and transformation, for both the change agent and those he or she is seeking to serve.

## Check the Car Before Pointing the Pistol

Barry Bailey tells of a son who worried greatly about his mother's safety. Fearing the worst, he bought the ninety-year-old woman a gun. Working with her tediously, he taught Mama how to use the pistol both correctly and boldly. As she was leaving her favorite shopping center one day, she found two men sitting in her car. Instinctively, Mama took out the pistol and pointed it right at the twosome.

Shouting at the top of her lungs, she exclaimed, "Get out of my car or I'll blast you away!" The men jumped out, slammed the door, and ran away as fast as they could. Mama promptly got into the car, put the key in the ignition—but nothing happened. And for good reason; she was in the wrong car. She tried to find the two men to apologize, but they were long gone![12]

Many church leaders point the pistol before checking the car; they fire off a volley of changes before carefully examining the make, model, and style of their congregation. Caring about culture is caring enough to see that the key fits before firing off in all directions; it's caring enough to link new initiatives to the legacy of those you seek to serve.

# CHAPTER 4

# MANY WORLDS, MANY SYSTEMS

*PRINCIPLE:*
*UNDERSTAND YOUR CONGREGATION*
*AS A COMPLEX SYSTEM OF SYSTEMS*

T homas Jefferson was a masterful agent of change. At numerous junctures in his life, he crafted key foundation stones for democratic philosophy and society. He made such a contribution by entering into all major spheres of nineteenth-century life. A visit to his mountaintop Virginia home, Monticello, reveals his varied and far-flung interests. Jefferson was active in the world of politics, of diplomacy, of science, of agriculture, of education, of business, of music, of exploration, and more. In addressing a gathering of Nobel Prize laureates at the White House, John Kennedy mused that no greater array of talent had gathered in the executive mansion—except when Thomas Jefferson dined alone.

Like Jefferson, the effective congregational change agent enters into the many worlds of congregational life. Acknowledging only one aspect of church life is not enough; accomplished agents of transformation need to move confidently within the varied spheres of congregational life.

These varied worlds or spheres are commonly called *systems*. Framed within the culture of a church, these centers of energy, activity, and influence propel congregations in either positive or negative directions. The true texture and fabric of a particular culture is not truly understood until you enter into the systems of that culture.[1]

## PRINCIPLE:
## UNDERSTAND YOUR CONGREGATION
## AS A COMPLEX SYSTEM OF SYSTEMS

# The Political System

The political system of a local church collects and channels the power of a particular group of people. Through both judicious and manipulative means, various individuals come into positions of influence which allow them to hold sway over the direction of the church. Let's look at both the layers and the players of the political system.

## *The Layers of the System*

Two layers or types of political systems function in most congregations: formal and informal. Formal political systems are easy to spot, since they are listed on the local church's official organizational chart: the vestry, administrative board or session; the moderator, church clerk, or designated chairperson.

Informal political systems, however, are more difficult to see. Tracy Tennant was candidating at a suburban Denver, Colorado, church for the position of senior pastor. The official search committee meeting went extremely well, so she assumed that there would be few surprises as the evening moved on. At the end of the meeting, however, Helen Yates, a committee member, motioned for Tracy to follow her; she indicated that there was one more member of the congregation Tracy needed to meet.

After driving to a modest home in the community, Helen introduced Tracy to "Mom" Reeves. "Mom," it turned out, was the matriarch of the congregation, the spouse of the founding "father," now deceased. The candidate and Mom chatted amiably for about thirty minutes, then Tracy was abruptly ushered out.

Turning to Helen, Tracy inquired, "What was that all about?"

"Oh," Helen responded, "there's no way we could hire a pastor without first checking with Mom. Relax, though: I think she liked you."

Who are the "Mom" Reeves in your congregation? How do you deal with them? In completing a research questionnaire for the Change and the Established Congregation Project, one respondent gave this advice:

When you make them into the enemy, you set up a dangerous dynamic. It's a lot better to make them into friends. Spend time with them, and help them understand your goals for the church. Solicit their advice. I don't mean that you play up to them in a way that gives them more influence than they should have, but just that you recognize what they have to offer.[2]

In addition to individuals, groups often constitute part of the unofficial power structure of a congregation. In established, traditional churches, adult Sunday school classes, for example, are a key "power" component, wielding impact and leverage. The experience of Pennsylvania pastor Jimmy Ross points to the class setting as a natural arena for conversation and influence:

People have a way of talking about what they want to talk about if there is a hot issue, regardless of what the Sunday school lesson might be on. They might well wind up discussing some of those issues on a Sunday morning, and those issues often are talked about at their fellowship functions. Nothing is brought to a vote, but you get a feel for where people are when you are in those discussions . . . and that has influence on the direction the church takes.[3]

What groups wield influence and set direction in your congregation? Sunday school classes, women's circles, adult choirs? What can you do to be in touch with such groups, in recognition of their role?

## *The Players of the System*

Participants in the Change and the Established Congregation Project underscored the transitional character of our time. Respondents both to questionnaire instruments and telephone interviews often spoke of shifting "players" in the political landscape of their congregation. Baby boomers, in particular, are no longer content to sit back and assume a passive leadership role; increasingly, they are knocking on the door of influence and power in churches. This is creating significant tension and challenge in the political system of congregations. One respondent put words to the "tug of war" in his heart and parish:

It's like I'm pastoring two different congregations. . . . Their expectations are so different. And the issue of change is the core one. The younger members want to see more contemporary worship . . . the older people don't want . . . the Sunday morning schedule messed with. I can understand [their point of view] but it leaves me feeling like I'm in a Catch 22 situation. I can't win, no matter what I do.[4]

But congregations can move through such tension. Ministry/nurture options can be multiplied for both generations. Differing generations can share power and leadership. Fred Bernhard's experience at Oakland Church of the Brethren illustrates this hopeful route. In five years' time, Bernhard led his congregation through a significant period of expansion, during which power shifted from one generation to the next. This was, in large measure, a response to Bernhard's forward-looking, dynamic, hope-filled vision.

The older generation at Oakland Church, Bernhard reflects, "didn't up and leave, they didn't dig their feet in, they willingly turned over the mantle." When asked why, he responds, "I think it was just because they are forward-looking people of faith and can see some of the potential. . . . Many in that group are still very active, still plugging away and doing what they can, but they do not try to be [in] power anymore."[5]

Savvy change agents are aware of the shift in players in church political systems, negotiating the transition of power with awareness, sensitivity, and great wisdom.

## The Transportation System

A second center of activity and leverage to consider is the transportation system of your congregation. The transportation system is the way your church moves things along, the way you facilitate (or stall) business, ideas, dreams, conflicts, problems, or possibilities. Most church transportation systems involve at least three components: process, structure, and communication.

### *Process*

Process refers to the way your church moves toward decision. For example, does your congregation allow members to give input into major decisions, or does one authoritarian leader rule the day? In research conducted as a part of the Change and the Established Congregation Project, over 85 percent of respondents affirmed the following statement:

"If a church is to change in pace with the times, then the decision making must be done broadly, so that most active members feel they have had a voice."[6]

Involving others in a decision-making process varies, however, depending on the scope of the decision. Issues involving the entire congregation (macro-issues), need, of course, to be resolved by the whole congregation. On the other hand, ministry-specific issues (micro-issues) need to be resolved by those most affected.

One respondent illustrates how appropriate decision making often becomes ironically twisted. In this individual's congregation, the leadership insisted that the whole church vote on the color of the women's restroom. Later that year, however, a Christian Education Director was hired without a vote of either affirmation or approval from the congregation.[7]

LifeQuest, a Fort Wayne, Indiana, research agency, recently surveyed more than 500 pastors, serving congregations ranging in size from 25 to 3,400 members. Seventy-seven percent of those responding registered an interest in simplifying or streamlining decision making, and 19 percent indicated that their congregations are either studying or currently modifying the way decisions are made.[8]

How does your congregation process micro and macro issues? What steps can you take to maximize your process?

## Structure

A related component of your congregation's transportation system is the structure of your congregation. The ability to process and move things along is directly affected by the way you are organized. Are ideas, dreams, and challenges expedited by your structure, or delayed? Are members released for ministry through your structure, or bogged down in endless committee meetings?

Irv and Nancy Heishman are copastors of an inner-city congregation in Harrisburg, Pennsylvania. In their leadership role, they found themselves attending more and more meetings, with little discernible result.

"[We became] stuck in that mind-set of just sort of doing what we always have done and not thinking very clearly about what is really needed in the life of the church," says Irv Heishman.[9]

The Heishmans and their congregation are in the process of developing a new structure, anchored to a vision statement. The resulting new structure will be reevaluated every three years, in light of the evolving vision of the congregation.

Along with a linkage to vision, effective church structure is shaped by a number of other key principles or maxims:

- Recognize that the world has changed; we no longer live in a churched culture, but an unchurched culture—thus an outreach mind-set is essential.
- When you operate with an outreach mind-set, you need to organize and structure for nimbleness.
- To achieve nimbleness, give a need to a leader, not to a committee, and allow the leader to organize his or her own action group to get the job done.
- Minimize committees. Steward your people's time in the direction of hands-on ministry, rather than theoretical discussion.
- Fly this banner high: Simple says it best. Too many well-meaning change efforts have fallen victim to the black hole of bureaucracy.

The restructuring of congregations for maximum ministry and outreach is a front-burner issue for churches. The degree of restructuring will vary from congregation to congregation; however, some variation on traditional organization needs to occur to assure an emphasis on mission, not maintenance. Form needs to follow function.[10]

## Communication

A last component of your congregation's transportation system is the communication prowess of your church.

In *The Kennedy Assassination,* Bradley Greenberg notes that within sixty minutes of President Kennedy's death, nine out of ten people in America were aware of the tragedy. Forty-two percent of the population heard about the shooting within fifteen minutes, and more than 70 percent knew within thirty minutes.[11] What is the rate of diffusion of information in your congregation?

Effective communication is the lubricant in the transit system of your congregation, greasing the process and structure of your life together. When good communication is operative, things move along briskly and well.

# The Resourcing System

The resourcing system is the way your church equips, "feeds," motivates, and supports its members. Congregations resource people in varied ways:

## *Caring*

At times, society can be incredibly impersonal and uncaring. The Department of Social Services in Greenville County, South Carolina, sent the following notice to Philip Fleming:

> Your food stamps will be stopped effective March, 1992, because we received notice that you passed away. . . . May God bless you. You may reapply if there is a change in your circumstances.[12]

People urgently need the caring embrace of congregations. Skillful pastoral care, notes of encouragement, phone calls of concern fortify both individuals and churches. Empathetic love replenishes in the midst of a consuming society.

## *Spiritual Development*

Linkage to the Spirit also fortifies the Body of Christ. Church renewal consultant David Young tells of encountering an overflowing bathtub. Instinctively, Young reached for a bathroom plunger and began plunging away. After working up a considerable sweat, he decided to stop and collect his thoughts. As he did, a new line of intervention came to mind: Check the drain release. Sure enough, the release lever was in the up position, rather than in the down position. It occurred to Young: It really isn't wise to plunge closed drains.[13]

Spirit-resourced churches and people avoid plunging closed drains. Through Spirit-prompted insight, they learn where the levers are in life, releasing murky prospects, opening themselves to springs of hope and promise.

Uplifting worship, spiritual direction, prayer teams, and Bible-study sessions all help leverage people forward.

## *Education*

At a "Church in the 21st Century" conference, South Carolina Baptist leader Reggie McNeil reminded his listeners of the high stakes related to education and knowledge:

1. Leaders can no longer rely on control and planning for effectiveness. The new requirement for leadership is to be prepared to meet any challenge.

2. Success is now dependent upon our ability to create new knowledge with our colleagues.

3. Mastery of the knowledge-building process is the competitive capital for 21st-century success.[14]

Effectiveness in adult education is a critical component of the resourcing system of your congregation. The availability of books, videos, expanded adult-study sessions, seminars, satellite learning opportunities, along with access to the "information highway"—all contribute to a healthy knowledge base across congregational life.

## The Weather System

The "weather system" encompasses those factors that influence the overall climate or emotional health of your church. At least three factors are key in the regulation of congregational climate: levels of extroversion/introversion, levels of anxiety, and levels of self-esteem.

### *Levels of Extroversion/Introversion*

The Myers-Briggs typology is one of the best known personality profiles in the world.[15] In recent years, this typology has been applied not only to individuals but to organizations. Though all four categories of the standard Myers-Briggs typology have relevance to congregations, the extroversion/introversion scale is of particular interest. The degree to which a church is introverted or extroverted has a significant influence upon its climate and weather system.

James A. Christopher, senior minister of First Congregational Church in Bloomfield, Connecticut, summarizes the major markings of extroverted and introverted churches:

## EXTROVERTED CHURCHES

- have more open boundaries and mixing of people and programs.
- can act quickly and think things out in the open on the go.
- take the spoken word as reliable communication.
- look outside for help when in trouble.
- express faith easily in public.

## INTROVERTED CHURCHES

- have a clear sense of space, territory, and boundaries.
- like to reflect inwardly and test thinking with their own group before acting.
- prefer written communication and documentation.
- draw a tight circle and look inside for help when in trouble.
- express faith more readily in one-on-one, personal context.[16]

No intrinsic value attaches to either extroversion or introversion. However, either influences change strategies significantly. Demonstrating sensitivity to preferred styles of life together in either the extroverted or the introverted church will do much to facilitate positive change and advancement.

### Levels of Anxiety

All congregational weather systems have a particular capacity for change. In varying degrees, churches will accommodate adjustments in routine and alterations to accustomed habits, but beyond a particular point, they resist. When this capacity line is reached, dark clouds and ominous skies form very quickly, as the weather system of a congregation goes from sunny to stormy.

When ominous conditions overshadow congregational life—either because of change, conflict, or crisis—research suggests that persons then (1) narrow their perspective; (2) narrow their trust; and (3) vent their anger toward third parties.[17]

What an organization desperately needs at such a moment is some breathing room. A key calling for the change agent is to be a nonanxious presence. As Edwin Friedman points out, clergy and other change agents can function as:

transformers in an electrical circuit. To the extent we become anxious ourselves, then when anxiety in the congregation permeates our being, it becomes . . . fed back into the congregational family at a higher voltage. But to the extent we can recognize and contain our own anxiety, then we function as step-down transformers, or perhaps circuit breakers.[18]

## *Levels of Self-Esteem*

The prevailing influencer of congregational weather systems is the confidence level of a particular body of believers. If confidence and self-esteem are high, the climate of a church is usually positive and attractive; if confidence and self-esteem are low, the climate of a church is usually subdued and less than inviting.[19]

Congregational self-esteem is often linked to the self-esteem of its members. A group of newly baptized members (properly dried and clothed) eagerly waited at the back of the church sanctuary to greet morning worshipers. One by one, persons filed by, but the majority had difficultly making eye contact with the new converts. Observing this tendency, the congregation's pastor found his "temperature" rising; he had spent months recruiting and cultivating these new people, only to find them now receiving the cold shoulder. Confronting a long-time attender with his anger and disappointment, he was taken aback by her response.

"Oh, Pastor," she replied, "it's not that I don't want these newcomers; it's just that I feel inferior whenever strangers are around."

How would you characterize the self-esteem of your congregation? In what ways can you bolster the identity of your people?

## A System of Systems

Undoubtedly, we could identify other subsystems. These categories, however, do summarize the four major centers of influence and energy found in local church reality.

With these subunits in mind, we turn now to their universal impact on congregational life. As they come together to form an overall congregational system—a system of systems—what principles or lessons emerge?

*The first lesson is that everything is a part of everything else.*

65

Board chair Glenn Thomas searched for a way to represent congregational life in a dynamic fashion; the standard linear, "boxy" organizational chart felt lifeless and anemic. While brainstorming with his wife, the idea of a mobile came to mind. Working all weekend, Thomas produced a finished product, just in time for the monthly church board meeting. Arriving early, Thomas hung the mobile—carefully, strategically—over the center of the board table. For the first ten minutes of the meeting, board members repeatedly glanced toward the swirling collection of shapes, sizes, and colors.

Seizing the moment, Chairman Thomas asked if they could read the labels on each piece of the mobile. Piece by piece, the board members identified each section of the mobile. Before long, all major arenas of congregational life were lifted up and acknowledged.

But Thomas' main point was yet to be made. Pointer in hand, he brushed aside one part of the art piece; the whole mobile swirled around, unbalanced.

"So with us," Thomas noted, "when we brush aside one part of our network of ministries and relationships. We too become tangled and imbalanced."

It is impossible to tamper with one subsystem within a larger system without tampering with other subsystems as well. As with a hanging mobile, when you touch one part of congregational life, you affect many other parts as well.

This truth often slips the minds of well-meaning change agents. For example, a Christian education director naively switched the time of vacation Bible school to a calendar date more available to community youth. In doing so, however, she bypassed Sadie Patterson, founder of the Bible school. Sadie not only had designed the format for the school, she also established a traditional time (third week in July) for the school to be held. Needless to say, a firestorm erupted when Sadie got word of the switch to a different week. The resulting controversy detracted from the well-intentioned efforts to reach community youth.

What happened in this instance? Among other things, an attempt was made to change the programming (the resourcing system) of the congregation without consulting the power structure (the political system) of the congregation; one part of congregational life was tampered with without the awareness that other parts of congregational life were being affected as well.

# Waking Sleeping People

A proverb warns that waking sleeping people is disturbing. So too with congregational systems: stirring complacent churches is disturbing.

*A second lesson in understanding your congregation as a complex system of systems is the principle of homeostasis. Literally, homeostasis means, "to stay the same."*

Biologically, we have many homeostatic mechanisms to control body temperature, the amount of light entering our eyes, and the level of salts, fluids, and blood sugars. When these mechanisms are disturbed, trauma comes to our physical systems, causing pain and disruptive stress.

So too for the system called the church. Within most congregations are a variety of thermostats that work to stabilize church life at certain standard, accustomed, "stay the same" levels. When disturbed, however, congregational systems—like bodily systems—resist, in the face of trauma and pain.

Our knowledge of this truth, however, is no reason to avoid changing congregational systems. It is simply a reminder that waking sleeping people is disturbing; stirring complacent, "stay the same" churches is troubling. As you upset the equilibrium of folks, move sensitively and with much savvy.

# Working Smarter, Not Harder

The system is designed for the results it is getting; if you want different results, you need to reconfigure the system. Ezra Earl Jones has led The United Methodist Board of Discipleship for many years. By his own admission, he had become quite adept at pushing himself and others to work harder and more furiously at the challenge of church revitalization. But then, Jones says, "One day a friend made a simple statement: 'The system is designed for the results it is getting. If you want different results, you have to redesign the system.' That statement changed my life."[20]

*A third lesson in understanding your congregation as a complex system of systems is that hard work—in and of itself—will change nothing if the system is broken or misaligned.*

Pastor Cheryl Banks agonized over the decline of financial giving in her inner-city congregation. In an attempt to resolve the issue, she sent a group of her finest lay leaders to a top-drawer seminar on stewardship. After arriving back in the parish, they poured their lives into the message of tithing and whole-life stewardship; bulletin inserts, moments of mission, four-color posters, and inspirational videos—all were utilized. But nothing happened. So the committee poured on more energy and effort; more information and motivation. But still nothing happened.

Calling Frank Zittle, her district superintendent, Pastor Banks vented her frustration. Zittle listened carefully, and at a timely moment, asked a probing question: "Cheryl, are you trying to raise money or people?"

The simplicity of his question reminded her that she had totally neglected the morale of her parishioners. In the process of trying to equip her people, Pastor Banks had battered them with too much programming; the "resourcing system" of her congregation was in overdrive, but the "weather system"—the basic confidence and spirit of her people— needed urgent attention.

There is an old saying: If the horse is dead, dismount. We often amend this phrase with our own revised standard version: If the horse is dead, buy a stronger whip . . . move the horse to a new location . . . appoint a committee to study the horse.

So, too, with congregational life. If part of our church life and system stops working, rather than dismounting and acknowledging the problem, we tend to keep going and going. God's call to us, however, is to work smarter, not harder—to stop the car and fix the tire, rather than drive on smoking rubber; to stop the process and correct the part of the system that needs attention.

Sometimes the entire system needs to be revamped. Futurist Alvin Toffler refers to the period between 1950 and 2020 as "a hinge of history," when the old is dying and the new is being born.[21] Given Toffler's prediction of radically shifting paradigms, some congregations are called toward a total systems overhaul.[22]

This is especially true for new congregations. It is ironic that much of new church development is actually the planting of old churches—old in terms of vision, structure, membership, and paradigm understandings. As we struggle with the reconfiguration—and in some cases the revamping— of systems in established congregations, new church plants could model helpful future approaches to structure and ministry.

# A Stream of Movement

Purposeless, status quo congregational life is like a stagnant pool; purposeful, vital congregational life is like a stream of movement. The "head" of the stream is the energy generated out of the vision of your congregation. Like a powerful current, vision draws people toward your church, channeling them into the life and systems of your congregation. Like the fins of a turbine, the political system, transportation system, resourcing system, and weather system of your congregation either move or impede people in their quest to find spiritual meaning. If they are operational and functional, the various subsystems of your church will encourage wholeness, eventually propelling persons toward mission in the world.

The outcome of such movement is transformation. Healthy, functional congregational systems change human lives. In her short story "The Whisper Test," Mary Ann Bird tells of growing up with a cleft palate and partial deafness in one ear. Rejected by most of her peers, she found a special acceptance in a second-grade teacher by the name of Mrs. Leonard. One day Mrs. Leonard gave an annual hearing test to Mary Bird's class. She conducted the test by whispering a different phrase to each student.

> Finally it was my turn [Mary Bird writes]. I knew from past years that as we stood against the door and covered one ear, the teacher sitting at her desk would whisper something, and we would have to repeat it back . . . things like, "The sky is blue," or "Do you have new shoes?" I waited there for those words which God must have put into her mouth, those seven words which changed my life. Mrs. Leonard said, in her whisper, "I wish you were my little girl."[23]

Healthy, effective congregational systems enable persons to hear God's whisper in their ears, and thus to hear new possibilities for wholeness and mission in the world.

What is the decibel level in your church system?

# CHAPTER 5

## THE LEARNING CONGREGATION

### PRINCIPLE: CREATE OPPORTUNITIES FOR INDIVIDUALS TO LEARN, GROW, AND CHANGE

Fellowship Church was a rural family chapel, disguised as a suburban community church. As an inexperienced but seminary-trained pastor, Lenny Harrison scrabbled for a pathway through the casual, unorganized folk customs of his people. Taking his church board chairperson, Waldo Miller, out to lunch, Lenny vented his anxiety, concluding his heart-cry with Action Item one: "For starters," he implored, "can't we develop a church budget?"

Waldo thought for a moment before he replied, drawing out his words with the hint of a southern accent: "Pastor Lenny, I don't think that really is necessary. I don't have a budget at home, and Sarah and I manage our pennies just fine. I think Fellowship Church can do just the same."

This lunchtime chat illustrates an important truth about congregational transformation: individuals change before churches do. If the people of your congregation are not stretching in their own personal lives, you will see diminished potential for stretching in their corporate life as the people of God. It's hard to persuade people toward new ways of managing money in the church, for example, if they are not stretching toward new levels of financial discipline at home.

*70*

## PRINCIPLE:
## CREATE OPPORTUNITIES
## FOR INDIVIDUALS TO LEARN, GROW, AND CHANGE

As we discussed in the last chapter, the *resourcing system* of your congregation is a key sphere of influence that affects overall church health. One crucial component of the resourcing system is education. As you expand the educational effectiveness of your parish, you augment the knowledge base of your people.

In addition—as we go on to say in this chapter—enlarging the learning character of your congregation enlarges your congregation's capacity for innovation and change. Though every congregation has a certain capacity for change (which, if exceeded, can produce spasm and significant anxiety), that capacity can be stretched and expanded significantly over time. Like a pair of tight jeans, a local church's capacity for new movement and direction can be stretched toward a new "fit" and feel for the future. A primary way to stretch a congregation's capacity for movement is through advancing the level of learning that occurs within your church.

## Traits of a Learner

Persons who are open to learning and new experiences often share these traits.

### *Childlike Curiosity*

Children move through the world with a wonderful inquisitiveness, exploring and experimenting at will. It is no coincidence that Jesus told his disciples that they would never enter the kingdom of God unless they became like children (Matt. 18:1-5). Christlikeness is akin to childlikeness; renewing and transforming the Body of Christ is linked to activating the intuitive, imaginative instincts of Christ's people.

One needn't be wild or overzealous in prompting the childlike, playful side of congregational life; effective strategies can be simple and nonthreatening. Christ Church in Carol Stream, Illinois, is a small congregation of thirty people, eagerly seeking renewal. One worship service addressed the familiar account of the woman anointing Jesus' feet with costly ointment (Matt. 26:6-13).

During the children's message, the storyteller illustrated her words by placing a dab of sweet-smelling hand lotion (reminiscent of costly ointment) on the hands of each of the children. But she didn't stop there. Turning to the entire congregation, she invited each worship participant to receive a dab of lotion. One by one, the children fanned out into the sanctuary, placing a portion of their lotion on the hands of an adult. Soon the entire room was filled with the aroma of sweet-smelling perfume—and a fresh connection with the biblical story.

## A Teachable Spirit

Persons who learn have an open, teachable tenor. They are not "set in their ways," but anxious for the input, discernment, and experience of others. Such a life stance is difficult to achieve in this individualist age. As Robert Bellah and company pointed out in their sociological study, *Habits of the Heart* (Harper & Row, 1985), more and more of us have retreated into a radically isolating "meism." Rather than being open to truth in the larger community, we have attempted to find ourselves through autonomous self-reliance. Such rugged individualism has led to stubbornness, detachment, and close-mindedness. "If anyone is going to find the path through life," we reason, "it is me, myself, and I."

Truth, however, is not discovered in isolation and haughtiness, but in community and yieldedness. Encouraging people, then, to be in relationships and groups is a key step toward building a learning organization/congregation. Relationships lead us to becoming more open to others and to ideas, possibilities, and strategies not normally included in our worldview.

Nurturing a teachable spirit creates an important fulcrum for lifting the level of learning in congregations.

## A Problem-Solving Attitude

Paul Murphy, the famous chess player, was once browsing through an art museum. As he did, he encountered a painting titled "Checkmate!" The painting pictures a young man playing chess with the devil. The young man is clearly distressed as he finds himself checkmated, with no apparent way out. Talking to a nearby guard, Murphy learned that chess player after chess player had studied the board in the painting and come to a similar conclusion: The young man was without options. Murphy decided to study the board himself, and he stared at the painting for more than thirty minutes. Suddenly, he pointed to the young man and blurted out: "You still have a move. You still have a move."[1]

Like Murphy, effective learners have the adeptness to reframe even impossible situations. Such a skill-set, in the words of British professor Charles Handy, includes the "ability to see things, problems, situations, or people in other ways, to look at them sideways, or upside-down; to put them in another perspective or another context; to think of them as opportunities, not problems, as hiccups rather than disasters."[2]

Effective learners are willing to study even checkmated situations, reframing life, looking for the overlooked move.

## *A Future-Friendly Outlook*

Rather than choosing a learning path through life, too many of us end the quest for knowledge at a high school or college graduation platform. Effective learners, however, opt for the long haul, signing on to be lifelong learners. The commitment to lifelong learning affirms that all of life can be lived with fullness.

As one ages, it is natural to feel a gravitational pull toward a cynical, negative, "what's the use" outlook. Effective learners choose, however, not to be victimized by life's realities, but to take responsibility for their lives and their futures. They search for new discoveries, in spite of cataract-blurred vision and arthritis-pained steps; they explore new options, in spite of unfilled dreams and broken promises.

# The Biggest Obstacle

Cynical, negative, "what's the use" attitudes are the biggest blocks to learning in most organizations and congregations. When persons honestly feel that all is for naught, that life is slipping south, that the worst is yet to be, they have little or no motivation to learn.

The taproot of cynicism, however, is not circumstantial but spiritual. Historian Richard Lovelace has studied congregational renewal for most of his professional career. He believes that many in the Christian community are plagued by deep-seated spiritual insecurity. On first impression, all appears to be fine, "but beneath the conscious level there is deep despair and self-rejection."[3] Instead of manifesting the traits of a learner—childlike curiosity, a teachable spirit, a problem-solving attitude,

73

a future-friendly outlook—the insecure Christian is dominated by skeptical and fatalistic thoughts, actions, and speech. It is Lovelace's conclusion that there is little hope for congregational learning and change unless spiritual insecurity is addressed.

Most change-agent pastors agree. In seeking to open up rural Fruitdale Church to new ideas, Pastor Martin Brown underscored the importance of spiritual discovery. Out of Brown's vision, a women's prayer group formed, made up of persons with a strong desire for change and growth. Meeting for more than five years, the group prayed earnestly and specifically for the spiritual vitality of the congregation. Out of their prayer life came a sense of new energy in the church, most pronounced in the appearance of new male leadership. Since the church had a small membership of mostly women, the positioning of more men in places of responsibility was a major turning point. Commenting on this and other developments, Brown reflected:

> I think two things are essential for change: first a love for God that comes out as a strong desire for personal and corporate change, along with a willingness to be changed at any cost; second, a willingness to wait on the Lord, the Holy Spirit, to do the things we can't do, but which we know are needed.[4]

What Martin Brown and other effective leaders have discovered is the importance of life change. Traditionally, churches have sought to produce either *informed* people (loaded up with biblical or theological knowledge) or *conformed* people (politically correct, in keeping with denominational norms). Dynamic, vital, learning congregations, however, seek to produce *transformed* people (supernaturally changed, rooted in Christ).

Dick Shreckhise is a change agent pastor located in Lebanon County, Pennsylvania. In recent years, he has led his congregation through a remarkable season of transformation and holistic growth. In listing the principles that have shaped his leadership, one is struck by their theological character:

1. The Gospel message changes people;
2. [The] greatest need in the world is not for more intellectual people, or skilled people, or more powerful leadership . . . but for "changed" people . . . ;

3. Concepts like grace, forgiveness, love, reconciliation, prayer . . . are not static concepts. They communicate growth . . . creative expression . . . [and an] invitation to a new "changed" way of living.[5]

United Methodist pastors Jim and Rinya Frisbie have found a practical way to bring Shreckhise's convictions alive in their congregation. Before most meetings, seven to fifteen minutes are set aside to share celebrations, concerns, and experiences of God. The goal: To make each group gathering or business session a faith-centered event. The pastors achieve this through asking a strategic question: "What evidences have you seen of God at work in your life this week?"

"People . . . look at you blankly like, 'What are you talking about?'" the Frisbies observe. "But after a while, people begin knowing that [question] is going to be asked, and they start looking . . . for evidences of God's presence in [their] life. People begin sharing things, neat spiritual experiences that they have had and they . . . expect to have, and I think that [outlook] began to transform, not only the committee meetings of the church life, but people's individual lives."[6]

Possibilities for creating a learning organization/congregation grow as persons truly believe that life can be unstuck, that things can be different. The heart of such transformation is a spiritual reality that grasps our lives, making us both secure and free—free to discover, explore, and roam wherever God leads.

## A Focus for Learning

People have a higher learning potential as they discover their life passion, talents, temperament, and spiritual gifts. Individuals do not easily open themselves to new ideas and possibilities if they do not see themselves as "players" in either present or future reality. Another level of cynicism peels away as they discover their unique profile as gifted, contributing members of the Body of Christ. They discover a motivation to journey through life with anticipation and purpose.

Irv and Nancy Heishman are inner-city pastors of a long-established, midsized congregation. Frustrated in their search for quality youth advisors, they began an emphasis on spiritual gift discovery.

"As persons discern their ministry calling," they reasoned, "perhaps new leadership will come forth." Among other things, they stressed the "sifting" role of spiritual gift development. "Rather than adding more to our 'plates,'" they emphasized, "a discovery of spiritual gifts helps us discern our *focus* as learners and leaders."

Before long, a couple approached the Heishmans and offered to be youth advisors. Reflecting on the experience, Irv Heishman remembers:

> They came to us and said, "You know, we heard what you were saying, and we really would love to be youth advisors. . . . How would you feel if we resigned from the Board and resigned as Sunday school teachers, and all these other things." And we said that would be great. . . . It has been just wonderful because they give very strong, capable leadership to the youth. . . . Their personalities and everything are just perfect.[7]

As the Heishmans' experience points out, spiritual gift discovery happens best in the context of relationship and community. Solo discernment through self-scoring questionnaires and inventories has its place, but gift discovery best happens in the midst of others. Pastor and author R. Paul Stevens has found that this occurs effectively in small groups:

> In small groups in which I . . . have been a part, we designate one night a year for affirmation. It takes a whole evening. We agree not to put a label on anyone, or even attempt to use the titles given in the three gift lists in the New Testament. Instead, we go person by person around the circle, and each member in the group is asked to finish the sentence (if he or she can), "Colin, you are a gift to this group in the following way . . ." or, "God works through you, Celeste, to minister to us in . . . ." Where there is genuine interdependence, this exercise is almost always a relational feast.[8]

These pastors have observed a direct connection between self-discovery and the possibilities for change in congregational life. Spiritual gift discernment—in community—is a valued catalyst for advancing the learning organization/congregation.

## We're All from Missouri

People change from passive spectators to active learners/leaders as they venture out of their own backyard and experience. Most church members are from Missouri, the show-me state; an openness to new reality or need is directly related to seeing that reality or need.

A pastor's spouse complained for months about the strong draft coming from the living room picture window in the parsonage. Her husband dutifully reported the problem to the chairperson of the Stewards Commission time and time again—but to no avail. Finally, his wife came up with a sure-fire solution. In the dead of winter, she invited that chairperson and his wife to the parsonage to dinner. The meal went famously, with everyone riding a crest of goodwill. After dinner, the pastor's spouse suggested that the group retire to the living room. Strategically, she offered the couch to their guests—the couch in front of the picture window. As a strong northerly wind blew through the holes and cracks in the window framing, the guests talked on amicably, but awkwardly. Along with experiencing a pleasant conversation, they were experiencing a learning point. Not surprisingly, a new picture window "suddenly" appeared at the parsonage within a few weeks.

If you want the congregation to give more generously to local hunger needs, invite a group of homeless persons to an outreach commission meeting to tell their story. If high-school programming requires more funds, set aside a time during a worship service for youth to creatively demonstrate their present and potential ministry. If you need a photocopier in the church office, invite the property chairperson to visit on "bulletin day," to witness the mess and inconvenience of stencil-based duplicating.

What learning points do you need to create for congregational members? Where is it important to do more than talk about needs; where is it important to help persons experience those needs?

## Going Over the Mountain

Along with experiencing needs, people also can experience new possibilities for the future. Many congregational leaders have no awareness of ministry models, other than those traditionally implemented in their home church. In a global, translocal society, too many parish leaders are caught in local, provincial patterns.

For many years, Joe Harding pastored a large congregation in The United Methodist Church. The period of most rapid growth occurred

77

after a group of youth and advisors journeyed over the mountain from their home in Richland, Washington, to Bothell, Washington, to experience a contemporary worship service. Transformed by that experience, the youth returned to Harding's parish with a vision for a similar service.

At first Joe Harding and other leaders resisted, but finally, says Joe, "We did it one Sunday, and it was so powerful that we started [a] contemporary service in addition to [our] eleven o'clock. In other words, we changed the style of the earlier service, and that service grew from an average of 400 to 700. We moved an average attendance of 500 to 1,100 in a few years, and then had to start a Saturday night service."[9]

All because a group of youth and advisors left familiar ground, went over the mountain, and caught a new vision.

Ways and means to take your people "over the mountain" vary greatly. Fred Bernhard, of Oakland Church in Gettysburg, Ohio, encourages his parishioners to venture forth by supplying them with a steady diet of reading material from books and newsletters produced by church-vitality leaders. Bob Kettering, a denominational executive, organizes bus trips to win support for various projects, such as new church starts. Kendal Elmore, of Green Hill Church in Westover, Maryland, invites church-vitality leaders into his congregation to conduct seminars. Jerry and Becky Baile Crouse, an experienced pastoral team, regularly include visionary guest speakers in their Antioch, Virginia, pulpit. Mike Overpeck, of the Community Church of Waterford, Indiana, encourages core leadership to attend key conferences on twenty-first-century themes.

Bill Longenecker, a church-revitalization pastor in eastern Pennsylvania, has an especially creative approach. In restarting Stevens Hill Church of the Brethren, he instituted a number of renewal measures, including a series of membership covenants. Among other commitments, people pledged to visit a different congregation once a quarter. Why? Longenecker and other leaders realized that at the heart of a new future for Stevens Hill, were new ideas, perspectives, and outlooks. One source of such innovation was the experience of other congregations.

How might you take your parishioners toward new vistas and ventures? What practical mechanisms might you employ to expose your people to new models for ministry?

# Third-Party Power

Along with new models, people learn through new mentors. Formally defined, a mentor is a personal advisor whose very lifestyle and personal influence "rubs off" on an individual or institution. Like an experienced coach, a mentor gets up close, taking personal, intense interest in your progress and growth.

Several options for securing mentors have emerged in recent years:

## *Teaching Congregations*

One of the newest options for churches are congregations that mentor other congregations. Pioneered by the Teaching Church Network, based in Minneapolis, Minnesota, this approach develops congregations that are healthy, future-oriented, and outreach-minded, through mentoring relationships with congregations that are purpose-driven, culturally relevant, and people-centered.[10] Commenting on this teaching-church strategy, Leith Anderson notes:

> The most powerful part of this approach is the impact of change on the whole church body, rather than just on the pastor. Because staff and lay leaders participate side by side, the quality and endurance of positive changes are multiplied.[11]

Some congregations have developed their own mentoring relationships, apart from formal agencies. A small-membership congregation in Linthicum, Maryland, for example, sought out a large-membership congregation in Frederick, Maryland, for assistance in developing their Sunday school. The Frederick congregation was delighted to help, sending teachers and resources for an all-day workshop, along with providing ongoing assistance by telephone.

Think of congregations in your immediate area or judicatory with expertise in particular arenas of ministry. Do any of the ministry strengths exhibited by these churches parallel needs in your own congregation? Have you considered approaching one or more of these churches to develop an intentional relationship?

As we approach the twenty-first century, congregations will increasingly harness the power of peer education and firsthand learning. One of the many variations of the teaching church concept might fit your situation and setting.

## *Consultants*

A more familiar style of mentoring is to contract with a professional congregational consultant. Usually well-credentialed through books, workshops, and word-of-mouth reputation, church consultants have the power to legitimize new ideas. In many cases, they are little different from a visionary pastor or lay leader, but find receptive, eager ears because of their third-party power.

While pastoring in Bloomington, Illinois, Bob Cueni turned around a 146-year-old congregation through the use of an outside consultant. As a result of a two-day visit, the consultant developed a parish enrichment plan for the church that produced 91 possible strategies for renewal.

"That became a five-year plan for us," Cueni notes, "and we would just pass that around to each new set of committee chairs . . . and they would start implementing whatever changes were there . . . and it worked!"[12]

Consultants are powerful teachers, attracting receptive audiences. Though the financial price tag is often high, the judicious, strategic use of outside third parties pays rich dividends for years to come.

## The Goal Is Empowerment

An experience of life-change and hope (in Christ), giftedness and purpose, new information and vision, mentors and models open life up toward a wonderful array of new options. A sense of new options, in turn, empowers people, the ultimate goal of any learning organization/congregation. As aviator Brooke Knapp once affirmed, "There are two kinds of people: those paralyzed by fear and those who are afraid, but go ahead anyway. Life isn't about limitation, it's about options."[13]

Our challenge is to create an environment so compelling that life opens up for people. So much in society closes life down, narrowing and hoarding options. The new community in Christ, on the other hand, breaks possibilities wide open, empowering folks to walk toward adventure and fulfillment in ways they hardly imagined.

Educator Steve Tobolsky tells of snow-shoeing with a fifth-grade class in the backwoods of Wisconsin. Led by Reid Lewis of Aventure Francaise, they were inspired by his tale of a fourteen-year-old boy named Bennett, who overcame great adversity by tapping deep into reservoirs of inner strength. Soon Tobolsky and his students, all novice snow-shoers, found themselves positioned at the top of an extremely steep, snowy hillside. Lewis then reminded them of Bennett, repeating the phrase the young boy had repeated in his time of adversity: *"Bennett, tu peux le faire!"* (Bennett, you can do it!)" One by one, Tobolsky and his crew repeated Bennett's phrase—substituting their own names—eventually overcoming their fears and reaching the bottom of the hill.[14]

A learning congregation empowers persons toward similar strength—in Christ—and new options for the future, no matter what the obstacles.

# CHAPTER 6

# Barn-Raising Believers

## PRINCIPLE:
## NAME NEEDS, INVITING OTHERS TO HELP DEFINE SOLUTIONS

I n the movie *A Home of Our Own*, actress Katherine Bates plays a poverty stricken single parent, desperate to remove her children from the vices of Los Angeles. Traveling north, the Lacey clan, as they were known, arrive in Idaho, where they convince a nursery owner to sell them an old shack. In the remainder of the movie, the mother painstakingly pieces the house together into a livable habitat—until a fire tragically destroys the wooden dwelling. All seems lost at this point.

Then a miraculous thing happens: Scores of neighbors stream onto the Lacey property with saws, hammers, nails, and lumber. In barn-raising fashion, they rebuild the house in a striking display of sensitivity, competence, and teamwork.

The specifics of bringing about change are much like a community barn-raising. With sensitivity to the culture and systems of our locale, we repair—even rebuild—various aspects of our ministry with skill, competence, and *teamwork*.

### PRINCIPLE: NAME NEEDS, INVITING OTHERS TO HELP DEFINE SOLUTIONS

Solo efforts to bring about change are almost always futile; team efforts are often very successful.

# Make the Status Quo Dangerous

Persons do not naturally gravitate toward one another or change. It normally takes some precipitating event or crisis to draw individuals into a life-changing, team effort.

Motivational speaker John Maxwell wisely reminds us that people change when they receive enough, learn enough, and hurt enough.[1] In our last chapter, we explored the first two elements of Maxwell's formula; in this chapter we touch on the third. The "hurt" Maxwell refers to is normally linked to some stress-producing event or crisis. In some instances, a full-fledged "barn burning" is required to spark change and team effort; in most cases, lesser levels of anxiety and strain are necessary—but some level of stress is usually required.

An intelligent but inexperienced pastor encountered a perplexing problem in his first pastorate: a small, fifty-year-old congregation, carrying a significant mortgage on its original building. The interest payments alone were draining the budget at the expense of program ministry. Upon presenting the problem to his board, the pastor got little response, in spite of numerous pleas for action. Desperate for a solution, he formulated a radical step: sell the debt-free parsonage. As a bachelor, he didn't need a three-bedroom house, and he argued that an extra piece of real estate for a debt-ridden congregation was an unnecessary luxury. Anxious to make his case, he contacted a real estate agent to determine a fair market value for the property. Then, with this and other background information in hand, he met with the Stewards Commission, confident he had cracked the code on the congregation's indebtedness.

Not surprisingly, the Stewards Commission's response was one of outrage; how dare the pastor take this kind of initiative, pursuing an absolutely ludicrous idea. Tension and stress between pastor and people escalated to an all-time high. But out of the turmoil came an amazing result: The Stewards Commission, fearful that the pastor might actually implement his plan, formulated its own plan, which eventually eliminated the congregation's indebtedness.

Business leader Sir John Harvey-Jones once commented, "The task of leadership is . . . to make the status quo more dangerous than launching into the unknown."[2] How might you do just that in your ministry setting? Creating a disconcerting action strategy, like the one described above, is an option; here are some others:

## *Distribute Accurate and Revealing Statistics*

Facts and figures often speak for themselves. An Indiana judicatory executive, for example, jarred his member churches into action by supplying each congregation with a wall chart that displayed declining worship attendance figures for the last five years. A California pastor rattled and raised his complacent flock by instituting a self-study on stewardship patterns over the last decade. What statistical or factual data might vibrate the life of your local church? What tools or strategies could unleash new and revealing information?

## *Ask Key Authority Figures to Name Reality*

Certain voices carry more weight than others in the life of a congregation. Utilize that weight to your advantage. Whenever one eastern Pennsylvania pastor wanted to distribute "wake-up call" information (news of a year-end deficit; a need for more Sunday school teachers, etc.), he first shared it with a group of key homebounds in the church. Within two hours, the information was out—and with convincing authority.

## *Allow People to Fail*

By nature, church leaders are rescuers and fixers; when people are in trouble, we come to their aid, and when problems are looming, we fix them. Congregation members will have little motivation to work toward change, however, if we continually patch up faulty structures, systems, methods, and traditions. A powerful catalyst for renewal takes place in the wake of a royal screwup.

Possibilities for a new electronic organ/keyboard loom larger when we allow the poorly maintained pipe organ to fail in the middle of the worship service. Possibilities for additional secretarial staff increase when the newsletter and meeting announcements no longer go out on time.

# Manage the Chaos

In crisis and chaos, the effective change agent is an effective building contractor. By guiding the congregation with a wise hand, he or she oversees people and events as they move through the strain of pain. This occurs as he or she casts a vision, names needs, describes options for movement, and reveals a plan for involving others toward a solution.

As general contractor, the pastor or lay leader is not deeply involved in all the details of the changes or solutions. Rather, the effective change agent focuses on the big-picture tasks named above (vision casting, need naming, etc.) and delegates more microtasks (bringing about specific changes) to other leaders in the congregational community. In a telephone interview, consultant Norman Shawchuck advised:

> If you are going to be a change agent in the church, don't get involved in every decision. . . . I teach my clients [to focus] on the one, two, three decisions that are really going to change the life and nature of this church [over a five-year period]. . . . If you want to be a change agent, save yourself for those one, two, three areas.[3]

## Specify the Big Picture

Though the wise change agent/pastor does not become involved in every decision, he or she does exercise at least two macroleadership functions: defining the tenure and parameters of committees/task groups working on specific change-oriented solutions.

### *Define the Tenure of Committees/Task Groups*

Change stirs up apprehension. This happens for multiple reasons, including the common perception of change as threat. You can reduce that threat by clearly identifying committees/task forces working on change strategies as ad hoc or pilot study groups.

As Ted Engstrom has affirmed, this designation, "not only raises the enthusiasm of those involved, but also relieves the threat to the rest of the group. After all, if it doesn't work with them, then obviously it won't be imposed on the rest of the group. People are not threatened by change that is taking place in others."[4]

By defining a committee/task force as a short-term, experimental group, you alter the common perceptions of its work; you also enhance its chances of being perceived as friend, not foe.

## *Define the Parameters of Committees/Task Groups*

The wise pastor or lay leader also determines the parameters or boundaries for committees/task forces working toward change. As United Methodist Pastor T. Mac Hood commented, "That has really been our success . . . to give people a task and then allow them to do it. . . .[I do, however, try] to establish the parameter—what needs to be done and when it needs to be done, help them in the first meeting to understand what parameters of the project entail, and then let them go with it."[5]

Setting parameters is necessary—in part, to head off a common mistake: trying to change too much, too fast, too soon. The familiar proverb is true: We overestimate what we can do in one year and underestimate what we can do in five years. General contractors know that well-built barns are constructed plank by plank by plank.

In guiding people toward a realistic pace of change, effective pastors and lay leaders follow these principles:

*1. Affirm that grandiose is not always grand.* Overambitious, big-time plans do not always serve the best interests of a local church. In many instances, small is beautiful, beneficial, and better. Management guru Charles Handy reminds us that it is often the seemingly insignificant things that alter life most profoundly:

> The chimney, for instance, may have caused more social change than any war. Without a chimney, everyone had to huddle together in one central place around a fire, with a hole in the roof above. The chimney, with its separate flues, made it possible for one dwelling to heat a variety of rooms. Small units could huddle together independently. The cohesion of the tribe in winter slipped away.[6]

Where do you need to build chimneys—rather than bonfires—in the life of your congregation?

*2. Affirm that a journey of many miles is taken in many steps.* Most of us overestimate what can be accomplished in a year and underestimate what can be accomplished in a decade. Most change efforts need to be undertaken step by step, plank by plank. Three years worth of change cannot take place in three months. But it can be broken down into a series of smaller incremental changes, each with a measure of achievement. For example, a plan to increase the Sunday school can be spread out over several years, with realistic yearly target goals for new classes and new students recruited.

For major changes, sequencing is important. A growing number of established congregations are adding worship experiences to reach the unchurched. These seeker-sensitive outreach efforts contain a number of innovative features, including contemporary music, drama, and a more relaxed leadership style. Many of these services fail because the planners introduce too many new elements at one time. An established congregation with traditional worship for the believer normally cannot move to an unconventional service for the unbeliever in a single step—even through a second service.

A sequence of multiple steps gives people time to adjust to each smaller change as it comes. For example, the service might move from purely classical Christian music to light contemporary Christian music. When contemporay music has become the norm, the worship planners might introduce drama. As the congregation becomes accustomed to drama, the service can move toward increasing informality, then to a growing, public passion for reaching unchurched people.

The sequencing and exact order of various change steps varies, depending on the innovation desired and the experience of a particular congregation. It is crucial that intentional sequencing take place, with new elements spaced and introduced over time.

*3. Affirm that one size does not fit all.* Congregations are often seduced by the notion that a successful change effort at one church (for example, in program, workshop, curriculum, or ministry approach) will automatically work in their church. This of course is a false assumption. Each congregation has its own unique identity and fingerprint, defined by its culture, systems, and temperament.

Church size also affects the programs and ministry approaches a leader should attempt. Arlin Rothauge, of the Seabury Institute in Evanston, Illinois, pioneered understandings of the linkage between congregational size and change initiatives. What follows is a modified form of Rothauge's basic typology of church size:[7]

- FAMILY CHURCH. *Size:* 0-50 worshipers.
  *Type of Change Preferred:* simple, common sense initiatives.
  *Delivery Vehicle:* informal, face-to face relationships.

- PASTORAL CHURCH. *Size:* 50-150 worshipers.
  *Type of Change Preferred:* modified or custom-tailored ideas and resources.
  *Delivery Vehicle:* informal to semi-formal settings, developed by a committee structure, guided by pastoral initiative.

- PROGRAM CHURCH. *Size:* 150-350 worshipers.
  *Type of Change Preferred:* "as is" or slightly modified ideas and resources.
  *Delivery Vehicle:* informal to semi-formal settings, developed by a significant committee structure, guided by pastoral initiative.

- CORPORATION CHURCH. *Size:* 350-500 and over.
  *Type of Change Preferred:* sophisticated, professional ideas and resources.
  *Delivery Vehicle:* semi-formal to formal settings, developed by a significant staff structure, guided by administrative board policy.

Rothauge's typology is particularly helpful in avoiding common sand traps, such as forcing highly structured programming on a relationally based, family church. One size does not fit all. New ideas and resources need to be adapted (or bypassed completely), depending upon the numerical proportions of congregational life.

*4. Affirm that addition is better than subtraction.* In a survey distributed as a part of the Change and Established Congregation Project, persons responded to the statement, "When possible, it is best to make changes by increasing options, rather than needlessly changing existing programs that people like." Over 89 percent of respondents agreed with that statement.[8]

Change happens best as we multiply people's options, rather than "pulling the plug" on cherished activities. Adding a Saturday morning small group for working women is preferable to disbanding the Tuesday morning sewing circle (no matter how gossipy that latter group has become!).

*5. Affirm that God's provision accompanies God's vision.* People of vision and faith move out into the deep with great conviction and courage. But we are often woefully unrealistic about the amount of time, energy, and money required to accomplish our dreams. The Bible clearly calls us to dream new dreams and see new visions, but it also calls us to count well the cost. Mindful of this wisdom, effective leaders challenge committees or task teams with a fundamental question: "Do we have the minimal resources necessary—in terms of time, money, people, and energy—to undertake this effort?"

For example, if a committee feels the pull of vision for a junior-high ministry, does it have the people power, the facility, the money to get the project off the ground? Who will provide music? Who will arrange for the set-up and take-down of equipment? Who will speak? Who will provide funds?

Asking such questions does not discount the importance of faith, risk, and ventures into the unknown; new ministries are seldom conceived with every detail, ramification, and contingency clearly in view. However, *something* needs to be in view regarding a basic way to support and sustain a new effort. The tension between vision and provision is inevitable, requiring maximum wisdom and discernment on the part of change agents.

## Involve Others

Effective change agents involve those most affected by an anticipated change. Findings from the Change and the Established Congregation Project underscored the importance of open, broad decision making in the life of the church. That same research also revealed a number of practical methods for including the input of others in a change process:

### Minisurveys

One research participant uplifted the value of surveying the congregation on a regular basis:

> You can overwork it, but I favor a lot of what I call mini-surveys or opinion polls . . . through the newsletter or Sunday-morning bulletin. I try to do that maybe two or three times a year. That way, we know how people feel about the major changes we might be anticipating. . . . We always publish the results of the surveys so that people know we took them seriously.[9]

### Cottage Meetings

Another research participant shared the success his congregation had with yearly in-home gatherings:

Our church has a very positive tradition—a series of cottage meetings every fall. Each person in the church is invited to one of these. The host family provides either a full meal or dessert. . . . If the board is thinking about introducing a new program, we use the cottage meetings as a time to encourage discussion. This gives us a broad range of input, without the formality of a congregational meeting. People have come to enjoy the cottage meetings, and attendance at them now includes about three-fourths of the church membership.[10]

## Listening Sessions

Still another research participant shared the benefit of a one-time listening session related to a particular issue.

[As we contemplated our building remodeling] . . . we invited the congregation to a "listening session." . . . We divided them into groups of about ten people, and addressed a series of questions about the future, and they all responded, and then we collated that information. When we went to the congregation [to announce the final plans for the remodeling project] we said, "As a result of what you told us you wanted, here is what we have done, and here is what will be happening." . . . We were trying to give ownership for the decision to the people who really helped us to go in that direction.[11]

# Especially Young Adults

The Change and the Established Congregation Project asked participants to respond to the following statement: "If a church is going to change in ways that attract people in their twenties and thirties, then it is important to have persons from those age ranges as part of the boards and committees of the church." Not surprisingly, over 91 percent of respondents agreed.[12]

Reflecting on his effectiveness in bringing about change in his Cleveland, Texas, congregation, Pastor Harry Vein underscored the role of younger and newer lay leadership:

We have gotten more laity involved in the leadership of the church than has ever been involved before, and it is not only more of the laity involved, but it is having a lot of the *younger and newer members of the church involved* in the leadership, and then some in the decision making of the church (italics added).[13]

So as you draw together planning committees, ad hoc groups, input sessions, and task teams, make a special effort to include people of the twenty-something and thirty-something generations. Given their sheer numbers, any changes must recognize the presence of young adults—or they will remain largely absent from much of congregational life.

## Moving Toward Decision

As you move toward a decision point for a particular change, consider the following four crucial leadership actions.

### *Choose Your Language Carefully*

Language is not a neutral reality, but a cultural component laden with meaning. Every congregation has certain trigger words that pump emotion into a discussion. A wise pastor or lay committee is alert to these words, avoiding them altogether or substituting synonyms.

Pastor Knox Talbert of Willow Bend Church has the ultimate "word problem"—his people become incredibly concerned at any mention of the word *change*. Talbert, however, has developed a powerful synonym; whenever he wants to speak of bringing about a needed change, he speaks of "updating our ministry."[14]

What are the inflammatory words in your church? What synonyms might you employ? What words do you simply need to avoid altogether?

### *Provide Choices*

People tighten up when they see their leaders tighten up. Do not "own" a particular change possibility too early in the decision-making process. Rather, present several alternatives for addressing a particular need, encouraging lots of give and take around various avenues. Whenever possible, allow persons to choose their own destiny.

For example, when outlining plans for the relocation of your physical plant, present two viable alternatives—Future One and Future Two. Future One could be a site located in a fast-growing suburb, surrounded by ample acreage, but within the boundaries of a large subdivision. Future Two could be a site adjacent to a major east-west thoroughfare, considered prime land by developers and business people alike. In presenting each choice, outline both pluses and minuses; be professional in your approach, linking each possibility to the vision of your congregation. Trust the Spirit to lead in the final analysis and vote.

## *Articulate the Benefits*

As you encourage people to address a particular needed change, talk up the positive outcomes of such a risk.

In his role as change agent, Presbyterian Pastor Dennis Burnett finds it important to make the connection frequently between a possible change and the benefits that could result:

> It helps a lot to do some motivating by saying . . . "these are the benefits that would come" [from the proposed change]. . . . I do this intention-ally. . . .Whenever something related to [the proposed change] comes up in conversation, I would say, "That is why it would be a good idea to do such and such."[15]

Social Action Chair Frank Jackson longed for his congregation to become involved in Heifer Project International, an agency distributing heifers, chicks, and other animals to strategic need areas around the world. When initially hearing his proposal, church board members could picture only one more fund-raising effort. However, as Jackson showed slides of Third World children receiving an ongoing supply of milk and eggs, hearts began to melt around the board table. Connecting the proposed change to positive results and benefits reassured his board members during the anxiety of decision making.

As you emphasize the benefits, illustrate how the proposed change advances the vision and values of your congregation. Make a connection between the proposed change and the history of your people. Give testimony to the ways the proposed change honors God and builds up the Body of Christ.

## *Suggest a Trial Period*

One of the most productive and positive ways of moving toward a decision is to suggest a trial period for a proposed change. Persons unready to commit to a permanent change more easily accept a short-term initiative with a designated checkpoint. For example, rather than advocate that the young-marrieds class abandon the adult quarterly permanently, suggest trying out an elective book study for a two-quarter period. Indicate that the class will evaluate its experience at the end of six months and make a recommendation regarding next steps.

The Change and the Established Congregation Project discovered that a striking number of survey respondents affirm that a "trial period" facilitates the introduction of innovation.[16] Such strategy, they noted, communicated the provisional nature of a particular change, along with the option to evaluate at a future date. In doing so, it also encouraged greater openness toward the new and a willingness to experiment.

The tactic of a trial period also benefits the change agent. Such an approach minimizes the risk or reputation factor of the pastor or lay leader. If the new initiative works, there is obvious gain and positive recognition. However, if the experiment doesn't work, the leader (and all those involved) lose nothing, as the new ministry ends at a designated point, and life moves on.

The effectiveness of the trial period approach cannot be overemphasized. It is probably one of the most powerful methods the clergy or lay leader can employ to bring about change. People will attempt amazing things when they know that new behavior need not be permanent and absolute.

## Timing Is Everything

In the early 1980s, Pastor James S. Flora attempted to lead his 900-member congregation toward a major building expansion; located in the fastest growing city in the state of Maryland, the congregation desperately needed additional seating for worship. Early on, he detected trouble; with a congregation full of contractors, building a new sanctuary was not going to be an uneventful pilgrimage.

Reflecting on that experience, he realized, "If I had pushed the idea then, I would have split the church." In the early 1990s, however, the congregation built a new sanctuary with little or no dissension.

"I didn't even bring the idea up again," Flora reflected. "It just seemed to emerge on its own."[17]

Jim Flora's experience illustrates that timing is everything. Even the best idea, pushed at the wrong moment, can be a disaster. Wise church leaders discern carefully when to call for decision and action. Follow these six pointers on timing:

*1. Never introduce a new idea and vote on it in the same meeting.* Always allow space between your initial presentation of the new possibility and a final decision. Allow people ample time to make up their own minds.

*2. Identify clearly the avenues for additional information and input.* Make people aware of the option of more give and take with you and other members of the appropriate committee. Keep facts and figures flowing.

*3. If people are opposed, meet with them individually.* Listen carefully to objections, reviewing the benefits of the proposed change as needed.

*4. Don't position yourself for a negative vote.* Avoid a decision or vote, at all costs, when the tide is taking your boat out to sea.

*5. If you sense that the tide is against you, do a reassessment.* Does the vision or goal have broad backing, or is it an idea that belongs to only a few people? You may need to broaden the support base before proceeding.

*6. When you sense that people are "with you," bring them together and move toward a positive vote.*

## Together

As the world increasingly spins out of control, the sons and daughters of God ride the globe as a peculiar people, attempting to move into some position of influence and sway. In this regard, the Christian Church is much like a few reeds growing in a river—sturdy, but seemingly small and insignificant. If those reeds gather enough other reeds, however, they end up changing the course of the entire river.

As an individual, the change agent is sturdy, but seemingly small and insignificant. Determined, he or she stands strong but lonely against the wind. Such a leader stance is noble, but self-defeating; it is only as we stand together that significant, life-altering change occurs. It is only as one sturdy reed bands together with other sturdy reeds that the course of a river is changed.

Are you standing with, or apart? Are you attempting to bring about change alone—or together?

# CHAPTER 7

# Bridging Toward Tomorrow

## PRINCIPLE: BE ALERT TO
## THE REALITY OF TRANSITION

Davidvid Murphy commuted from Annapolis, Maryland, to Easton, Maryland, daily for seven years. Every day he crossed the Chesapeake Bay Bridge, the only quick access from Annapolis across the bay. One spring David's wife suggested that he and the rest of the family experience his commute from a different angle.

The annual Chesapeake Bay Bridge walk was only a week away, Susan Murphy reminded her husband. "Let's take part!"

And so the Murphys packed up bright and early on Saturday morning and headed for the bay bridge. After joining thousands of others, they hiked the five miles, enjoying stunning views of weathered lighthouses and multicolored sails, along with refreshing scents from spring breezes and bay currents.

After completing the walk, Dave Murphy turned to his wife and remarked, "I have driven this bridge for seven years, but never paid much attention to it. You know, there's a lot here—plus it's much longer than I ever realized. Much longer!"

Most change agents drive hard—away from the old reality toward the new reality, the new creation God has called us to envision. Unfortunately, many of us underestimate the scope and distance in between. Like David Murphy, we barely acknowledge the bridging experience between destination points. We assume you can get from point A to point C without ever dealing with point B.

## PRINCIPLE:
## BE ALERT TO THE
## REALITY OF TRANSITION

For many years, even social scientists gave little credence to the reality of transition. Through the pioneering work of William Bridges and others, however, we now know there is much to consider regarding the in-between time, the bridging experience between old and new.[1]

## Change and Transition—They're Different

Change and transition are not synonymous. Generally speaking, change is an external reality, while transition is very much an internal reality. For example, the *change* from Buffalo, New York, to Salt Lake City, Utah, can be completed in a few days—by loading a moving van, driving a series of interstates and toll roads, unpacking scores of boxes, sending out change-of-address cards, and showing up at a new job.

Making the *transition* from Buffalo to Salt Lake City, however, requires weeks, even years. When you change from one locale to another, you unpack boxes; when you transition from one locale to another, you unpack memories, emotions, dreams, self-perceptions, relationships, and even faith. Transition touches all aspects of our personhood; it challenges us to stretch from a familiar reality to a fresh, but frightening context.

## Where Are the Endings?

A wise pastor in east Texas once remarked, "Transition begins when you identify the endings."[2] In order to embrace something new, we often must say good-bye to the old. If a church starts a new, exciting summer Sunday school program, it does well to acknowledge that at least some persons will miss the prior program—even if the new one is a great improvement.

Some changes appear positive for everyone. If a Sunday school classroom has dirty, poorly fitting draperies and paint peeling from the walls, then new drapes and new paint—of a similar color—will please virtually everyone. But if the new paint is a significantly brighter color, some persons will undoubtedly miss the previous color (conveniently forgetting that the paint was peeling!).

In reality, most change stirs some feeling of loss. Even when we abide by the maxim that change is best accomplished by addition, not subtraction, some grieving is inevitable. Consider the predicament of Lakeside Church's Chancel Choir. Though they have not been replaced by the new Praise Ensemble, longtime members of the choir will nevertheless experience an emotional tug of war. For fifteen years, the Chancel Choir has been the adult choir at Lakeside Church, featured front and center every Sunday. Now there's a new element in the mix and choir members aren't sure what to think.

"Do we really want to share our spot on Sunday mornings?" some ask. "What if the new group is viewed as better than we are?" others question. "Maybe we are being pushed aside," still others muse.

Most change results in some measure of distraction, discontinuity, and even disorder. Out of such bewilderment develops a sense of melancholy, anguish, and eventually loss.

## Levels of Loss

The severity of the grief depends upon the level of loss involved. Changing the entire organizational structure of a congregation, for example, is in one category or level of loss, while changing the color of carpeting in the pastor's study is in a different category.

Levels of loss are linked to the level of change being attempted in a congregation. Change theorists often refer to two distinct levels or classifications of change.[3] First-level change involves activities or events that bring about improvement (introducing a new element) or adjustment (altering an existing element). Changing the color of carpeting would be in this category of change.

Second-level change involves activities or events that bring about revisioning (reconfiguring a significant slice of congregational life) and re-creation (reconfiguring the whole of congregational life). Changing the entire organizational structure of a congregation would be in this category of change.

Most change attempted in congregational life is in the area of first-level change. Many leaders in traditional, established congregations consider themselves fortunate if members are willing to accept various improvements or adjustments in church life. However, our ultimate goal should be some entry into second-level change—into a revisioning process that introduces, among other things, new values into a congregational system. As we affirmed in chapter 3, the most common mistake change agents make is to introduce a new program or ministry without introducing a new or accompanying value. Introducing new values is a difficult, painful experience—a second-level change experience. And if we can avoid pain, loss, and adversity, most of us—understandably—opt in that direction.

The gospel itself, however, as missiologist George Hunsberger reminds us, can be a source of pain:

> All change is perceived as loss. Loss precipitates responses of grief. While the gospel is a consoler and healer in the midst of loss and grief, it is also an ingredient in the life of the church that disturbs the status quo, stirs change, and heals by producing the pain associated with grief.[4]

Hunsberger goes on to say that our tendency to avoid pain might actually result in avoiding the gospel. Though taking Hunsberger's logic to extremes leads to a morbid, graceless life, it is a helpful reminder that pain and loss are not necessarily negatives; they also can be important catalysts toward change, growth, and greater obedience.

## Grappling with Grief

Given the fact that pain is not necessarily a negative, how does one deal with it in the process of change? As church members are reckoning with the start of something new, how does one grapple with the grief? Consider these six suggestions:

### *Don't Deny the Pain*

Don't speed across the bridge, slighting the scenery. Acknowledge the fact that people are disturbed, even hurting. Also acknowledge that such reactions are to be expected and are part of the process. Provide opportunities for people to name their sorrow, ventilate their anger, and acknowledge their grief.

In some cases, it is appropriate to identify with group or individual pain in some tangible way. A dramatic example of such a connection happened in a western U.S. classroom in the early nineties. A high-school student contracted cancer; in the course of his subsequent treatment, all his hair fell out. In a show of solidarity and support, all his classmates—along with the teacher—shaved their heads as well.

How might you identify with those caught in the pain of transition? Perhaps it means showing up in the Altruistic class as its three remaining members grapple with the pain of merging with another Sunday school group. Perhaps it means helping out at the associate pastor's yard sale as he or she prepares to move after a painful termination. Demonstrate that you are aware that people are hurting.

## Respect What Has Been

Show regard toward that aspect of congregational life being changed. One of the common mistakes change agents make is placing a negative value on the old and a positive value on the new. For example, it is tempting to mock the traditional nominating committee process and applaud the creation of a gift-based ministry emphasis. Lay folk, however, pick up such arrogance a mile away. And then we wonder why the gift-based ministry emphasis shrivels and dies on the vine.

In fact, the new is not better than the old; the new is simply more relevant than the old—but only for a span of time. At some point, even the most revolutionary idea will be old and irrelevant. So treat any current irrelevancies with the same regard you desire for your current—but someday irrelevant—project.

One tangible way of showing regard for the past is to recognize or even celebrate its significance. When the Henry Avenue Church needed to "transition" a loyal worker out of her long-term role as church secretary, the board chose also to celebrate her twenty-three years of service. After an appropriate "cooling down" period, they arranged for a time of recognition as part of a morning worship service, followed by a festive luncheon. A new beginning was clearly in view, but years of dedicated, loyal service were not ignored.

What endings do you need to recognize in a tangible, even festive way? What aspect of your congregation's past do you need to honor and lift up in high regard?

## Speak of the Problem, Not Just the Solution

A true visionary not only helps people connect with tomorrow's possibilities, he or she also helps people connect tomorrow's possibilities with today's problems. Most of us need to be constantly reminded of why we have embarked on a new adventure. That is why you often find pictures of overweight people on the front panels of refrigerators. At the very moment when we yearn to give up, we need to be reminded of the problem; we need to be reminded why we are suffering such grief.

When Sara Jamison complains of the dust and noise coming from the sanctuary renovation, remind her that she is crowded out of her favorite pew two Sundays out of four. When Joe Pepper gives you grief for orchestrating the move of the men's Bible class in order to make way for a larger baby nursery, offer to serve as tour guide, walking Joe through bunched up cribs and an obstacle course of toys and puzzles. On the path toward change, help people recall why they are making the journey.

## Expect Overreaction

Feelings of grief and loss can result in feelings of frustration and anger. When such emotions reach overdrive, it is easy to jump to conclusions and expect the worst. For instance: The revamped evangelism emphasis will lead to a takeover of the church by total strangers; the newly formed Alcoholics Anonymous group will wreck the fellowship hall and attract derelicts to the church property.

The remedy for overreaction? Hang in there with people; expect to be a shock absorber at times. Like a policeman on parking patrol, or an umpire at homeplate, anticipate the rage of persons who have just lost a measure of their self-definition. Try to stay poised and objective. Listen carefully, and clarify misunderstandings. Affirm that you really do care and want to help. Resist returning anger for anger.

In addition, explain carefully the limits of an evolving change, along with the next milestone in the process. Reiterate that the innovation in question is not forever, but subject to review and further consideration. Help distraught individuals visualize the boundaries around a new ministry or project. The air begins to leak out of anxiety's balloon when people sense that there is an evaluation date or checkpoint in the not too distant future.

### Provide a Piece of the Past

Chicago Stadium was a place of great tradition. Not only was it the home of the world champion Chicago Bulls, it was also remembered as the site of national political conventions, the Ringling Brothers Circus, and world-class ice hockey. The demolition of Chicago Stadium to make way for the new United Center was a traumatic experience for hundreds of fans. Wisely, the owners of the stadium decided to make available pieces of the "old barn" (as it was affectionately known) as mementos and souvenirs. Fans willingly paid the asking price for seats, floorboards, and bricks—thousands of bricks—as a way of connecting with the past.

Grieving church folk also need to connect with the past. Whenever possible, make available some literal or symbolic sign of what has served the congregation so well for so many years. If you are renovating the building, make available pieces of the old facility or selected furnishings; if the church preschool program needs to disband, present the director and teachers with pens engraved with the name of the school and its tenure of service; when new hymnals arrive, make available copies of the old songbooks. One congregation, for example, commissioned collectors' plates picturing their old sanctuary, and sold them as part of the fund-raising for a new building.

What mementos of the past might you provide as you move toward change? What aspects of legacy need to become tangible and passed on?

### Get People Involved in the New

The most effective and caring strategy for helping folks grapple with the grief of change is to get them invested in the new. Persons normally become invested when they become involved.

For a number of years, the Reverend Jenny Jackson-Adams pastored Morningside United Methodist Church in Americus, Georgia. During her tenure, the congregation experienced dramatic expansion, largely through an influx of unchurched persons.

During a period of especially rapid growth, one of Jackson-Adam's lay people, Jack, confronted her: "I'm getting to feel like a stranger in my own church."

Responding, Jackson-Adams said, "I'm just glad we are going to talk about this." And so they did. Jackson-Adams sensed that Jack was too far removed from the faces and stories of growth. She began to use him more as an usher, placing him in situations where he could meet new folks on a regular basis.[5]

Strategies for involving folks in the new, of course, vary. Some congregations intentionally balance the number of long-term and new members on boards and committees, to ensure that no category or constituent is forgotten. Other churches strategically utilize social events to mix newer and older members. Still other parishes employ assimilation teams or "undershepherd" systems to spot disgruntled members, taking initiative to invite them into a specific role or task. Bottom line: Don't let hurting people stew; get them involved in new opportunities for relationship and ministry.

## Warming Up at Different Temperatures

People move through discomfort and grief in different speeds and styles. Everett M. Rogers, in his classic *Diffusion of Innovation*, identified five categories of response exhibited by persons in a change process.[6] What follows is a slightly modified version of Rogers' findings and groupings.

First are the pacesetters. These are pure visionaries, venturesome types who dream new dreams at the drop of a hat. Often they are not in official, ongoing roles, but on the edge of congregational life. Normally, no more than 2.5 percent of the membership of a local church is made up of such people.

Next are the early adopters. These are individuals who quickly embrace innovative ideas. They are every change agent's dream, as they readily acknowledge the logic of blazing new trails. Often they are serving in key leadership roles and are widely respected. Expect about 13.5 percent of your congregation to fall into this grouping.

A third category is the middle adopters, a significant slice of the typical congregation, about 34 percent. These are individuals who watch carefully which way the wind is blowing. They can be swayed either by those proposing change or by those resisting change. Serving in roles throughout the church, these persons generally support a new direction, if the case for that direction has been well made and its proponents have clearly done their homework.

A fourth category is that of the late adopters. These individuals often vote against proposed innovations, but later support them, if the majority of the congregation moves in a forward-looking direction. They are skeptical and cautious by nature and make up another 34 percent of a local church.

A last category is that of the footdraggers. Comprising about 16 percent of your congregation, these are the last persons to jump on the change bandwagon, if in fact they ever do. They are highly resistant individuals, bound to traditional ways of thinking. These persons can be prone to sabotage innovations after they have been approved.

Take a few moments now to think of a recent innovation in the life of your church. Do you have it in mind? Now, think of the people of your parish. Can you visualize persons who fall into each of the categories named above? Who are the pacesetters, the early adopters, the middle adopters, the late adopters, and the footdraggers in your congregation?

Understanding these various speeds and styles helps leaders bridge the transition from the old to the new. Among other things, such understanding can relieve change agents of any illusion that everyone can be brought along on the journey toward newness in the same way, at the same time. Knowing the various speeds and styles for adopting change can also help leaders focus their energy during a transition time. Pacesetters and early adopters need little grief care or sensitivity during such a period; on the other hand, middle and late adopters need special attention.

Ohio pastor Eric Anspaugh acknowledged the problems that result when one fails to recognize the various ways in which persons adopt change. In the late 1980s, Anspaugh and one of his deacons, Harold, attended a Stephen's Ministry workshop. Returning to their congregation "pumped up," they were convinced that their deacon body could transition readily toward a Stephen's Ministry-style shepherding program. Says Anspaugh:

> We thought that it was such a good idea that all the deacons ought to just go right along with that, and I basically just pushed it right through, and had Harold's blessing. . . . But I failed to realize at the time that [though] some of the deacons were really excited about that, some of the deacons didn't want to have anything to do with it, but they wouldn't say that.[7]

Eric Anspaugh's assumption is a common assumption among change agents: If it is a great, logical, Christ-honoring, church-enhancing idea, everyone will just go along with it. Sixteen percent probably will. However, as the five categories of change adoption remind us, 84 percent of any given congregation (or deacon body) will need to warm up to the idea, in degrees, over an extended period of time.

## Acting on a Shaky Stage

Anthropologist Charles Kraft compares the process of change and transition to that of a shaky theater stage.[8] Much of life is "performed" on solid, secure, and familiar platforms. But the moment comes when we are called to step out into new territories and temporary platforms. Such an experience brings ambivalence, instability, and large doses of trepidation.

In some respects, such emotion just goes with the territory of transition; you can't lead people to the security of the promised land without first going through the wilderness. Even the wilderness, however, includes manna and oases. Provide respite for people, even in the most righteous and noble change effort. As the stage is shaking and the bridge swaying, provide sure footing and the experience of safety.

More than two decades ago, Alvin Toffler referred to these safe spaces as stability zones. To Toffler, a stability zone is marked by valued relationships or routines that are carefully maintained in the midst of certain change.[9]

### *Relationships*

A network of comfortable companions is one of the warmest security blankets. As the story goes, a donkey once entered the Kentucky Derby.

When asked, "You don't expect to win, do you?" the donkey replied, "Of course not. But the company's good."[10]

Intense levels of transition and change are less threatening when an individual (or a donkey, for that matter!) has strong social support.

Beyond personal, individual friendships, participation in a small group contributes greatly to the cultivation of positive relationships. For that reason, *the wise change agent multiplies the number of small-group opportunities during a time of transition.* Remember, small groups come in many shapes and sizes: Bible-study groups, twelve-step groups, caring groups, covenant groups, adult Sunday school classes, women's fellowship groups, men's fellowship groups, youth groups, and choir groups. The critical thing is to bring people into face-to-face settings, where they can experience love, support, and continuity during a time of discontinuity.

## *Routine*

A denominational executive was transporting his father home from The Johns Hopkins Hospital in Baltimore, Maryland. Suffering from liver cancer, the seventy-nine-year-old man was well aware of the crisis stirring within his life. As they left the hospital, the son turned to his dad and suggested that they take the new expressway out of town. The father objected fiercely. It was Old Forty (the traditional route out of town) or nothing, the dying man declared. And so, father and son crawled out of the city, stoplight after stoplight, traffic snarl after traffic snarl.

In troubling transitional times, routine is important. Using familiar roadways, following standard schedules, employing traditional menus is reassuring when the very foundations shake. Translated: *During change and transition, leave some things the same.* The first Sunday in the new sanctuary, don't tamper drastically with the customary order of worship; when announcing the new adult elective class, use the familiar Christian-education "spot" in the church newsletter.

According to organizational psychologist Edgar H. Schein, "Probably the most difficult aspect of initiating change is the balancing of painful disconfirming messages with reassurance that change is possible and can be embarked upon with some sense of personal safety."[11] Though difficult, achieving such balance is vital to effective transition. The provision for routine and stability zones of relationships contributes greatly to the equilibrium necessary for fruitful change.

## Turning Doubt on Its Head

Shaky stages, swinging bridges, and lonely wilderness experiences inevitably lead to doubts, often expressed in negative, murmuring words. Effective change leaders do not parrot such doubt, but turn it on its head. The *Executive Galley Catalog* suggests these positive replies to some complaints:[12]

| | |
|---|---|
| "It's not going to get any better." | "We'll try it one more time." |
| "We don't have the expertise." | "Let's network with those who do." |
| "There's not enough time." | "We'll evaluate some priorities." |

Learning and repeating a positive reply will do much to move you and your people through the murmurings of transitional, wilderness times.

An anonymous poem captures well the possibilities of in-between times and the new life of shaky, uncertain seasons.

> All growing is changing from one state to another.
> Leaving a world behind, entering the fear of the unaccustomed:
> of colors that don't blend, of holy words that jar,
> of fractures that give rise to visions.
> We have left one realm but have not yet arrived at the other. . . .
> That is the changeover in which we experience
>     our nakedness to the point of hurting.
> But there is no real growth
> without leaping,
> without crossing bridges and
> standing wide-eyed and
> shivering on a new shore.

(Adapted from a worship bulletin provided at the 1995 National Staff Consultation of the Church of the Brethren, Lake Geneva, Wisconsin)

# CHAPTER 8

# THE RIGHT START

## PRINCIPLE:
## LAUNCH CHANGES WELL

E very indicator suggested that January 28, 1986, was going to be a spectacular day. The unseasonable frigid weather of the early morning hours was dissipating as the expectant, enthusiastic crowds of spectators gathered. The moment for liftoff finally came, and the spacecraft blasted off the launchpad with fury. Up, up, up it went into the heavens with symmetrical beauty. Every eye within a twenty-five-mile radius strained to see the fiery, multicolored splendor. But then something went tragically wrong; instead of separating on cue, the rocket exploded, and the space shuttle *Challenger* crashed into the sea.

Well-intentioned change efforts normally fly quite well. As anticipation and expectation ride high, we have every hope for a smooth takeoff. But on occasion something goes tragically wrong, and the picture-perfect blastoff ends in an explosion. Fortunately, a change agent can usually prevent such explosions with forethought and a spirit of intentionality.

## PRINCIPLE:
## LAUNCH CHANGES WELL

We have examined the principles that precede this chapter for a reason: Unless certain foundation stones are in place, we will have difficulty in constructing an effective launchingpad for even the most noble change effort. Unless we and our congregations are in a learning mode; unless we articulate a clear vision; unless we understand culture and systems; unless we build a spirit of teamwork and togetherness; unless we are sensitive to the reality of transition—the rocket of innovation might just explode. The material that follows builds on all that has preceded it; the seven principles we have already considered are foundational to the hope of launching well.

## Plan Your Work, Work Your Plan

Church folk are great at brainstorming, but often lax at implementation. Given the voluntary nature of the faith community, an absence of follow-through might be expected; however, when credible dreams are left on the loading dock too often, people stop thinking in new directions. As Burt Nanus has observed, "There are few things sadder for an organization than an exciting vision that is poorly implemented."[1]

The antidote to lax implementation is disciplined intentionality: consciously executing your vision in measured steps. Intentionality comes to flower through action planning, a process in which next steps are plotted out. Action plans vary in their complexity, all the way from a few steps sketched on the back of a napkin to fully developed strategic plans. But in all cases, they answer five central questions:

1. What are we trying to accomplish? (AIM)
2. How will we bring it about? (ACTION STEPS)
3. Which resources are required? (RESOURCES NEEDED)
4. Who needs to be involved? (FOLLOW-THROUGH PERSON/S)
5. When do things need to happen? (BY WHEN)

As you answer these questions, remember to:

### *Be Specific*

Spell out exactly what you want to do—when, where, and how. Don't assume anything. If you intend to paint the children's nursery blue, for example, stipulate directly that you want to paint the children's nursery blue. As researcher Thomas Harvey has commented, "Too often, change efforts fail because members of a group have different presumptions about what they want to accomplish."[2]

## Be Realistic

Look at your aim through the lens of pragmatism, not idealism. This is especially important when it comes to timetables. Think of the approximate number of days it will take to accomplish a task—then multiply by three. List that date as your deadline. You will promote far better morale if you finish ahead of schedule than if you continually miss announced target dates.

## Be Brief

Wise planning is important, but don't be caught in the paralysis of analysis. In a telephone interview, Presbyterian pastor Jim Hodge reflected on his congregation's obsessive-compulsive bent toward planning.

"We spend an enormous amount of time on planning," Hodge admits, "and sometimes I have the feeling that there is a real reluctance to move ahead because . . . maybe we can plan just a little bit more. . . . At least in this church, it seems like a mighty slug moves the church of God."[3]

Remember: simple says it best. In strategizing and developing your action plans, be brief, be done, and be gone—implementing your dreams with vigor.

# Who Are the Legitimizers?

Because new efforts tend to be suspect, they need to be legitimized. One or two persons have the power to make a new idea permissible and acceptable in a congregation.

A large-membership church in the Shenandoah Valley of Virginia moved cautiously but deliberately toward a building relocation. They held a series of planning meetings, including one with a church-development consultant. In the course of her time with the congregation, the consultant attempted to make the case for relocation on the basis of mission and growth. A new location and an enlarged building, she argued, would give the congregation additional opportunities for holistic outreach and new-member ministry. The body language around the table, however, signaled that she was not making her point. Then, from a corner of the room, a hand went up; it was Ben Jones, a longtime leader in both the local and the wider church.

"This vision for growth is not unlike the vision we had for relief and service at the end of World War II," he began. "Tackling that dream seemed awesome, too, but we did it. I, for one, am tired of all the talk. Let's build!"

With those words, the mood in the room shifted from suspicion to support; a valued voice had spoken and blessed the new direction. As Lyle Schaller points out:

> Rarely is it possible to persuade everyone to support a new idea simply by lifting up the merits of the proposed change. At least one-third and perhaps two-thirds of the members will be influenced more by the opinion of these legitimizers than by the content of the proposed change.[4]

Who can bless and legitimize direction in the life of your congregation? A wealthy business owner, the chair of your administrative board, a well-respected young adult, the veteran church secretary, a matriarch or patriarch of long-standing? Look to these individuals not only to develop direction, but to sanction direction as a change effort is launched.

## Quick Wins

The launch of any change effort accelerates with signs of success and movement. A common leadership error is to bank only on long-term results, rather than attempt quick wins as well. Both are necessary in an effective implementation process.

Anxious to make progress in the quest for renewal, pastors Jim and Rinya Frisbie encouraged their northeastern Oregon congregation to do more than gripe about the absence of children and youth.[5] Begin by being the church you are, the Frisbies admonished, rather than lamenting the church you are not. Members of the congregation took them literally, addressing a troubling obstacle in their life together—cold pews (resulting from a faulty furnace).

"Little ladies who never wore slacks to church," Rinya Frisbie observes, "would freeze. And so [the ladies of the church] made some little pads to sit on . . . so the ladies could come and put them wherever they were going to sit."

The result of these and other "little changes" was remarkable, resulting in an influx of retired folks from the community and, eventually, young families as well.

For United Methodist pastor T. Mac Hood, the "quick win" for vitality was not pew warmers, but the church coffeepot. He explains:[6]

> The church didn't have any money, they were broke. I got several groups to buy a coffeepot, and it cost $155. They said, "We can't afford it." I said, "Well, let's get several classes together and buy it." And we got it, and the whole congregation now feels good about it. It is a nice, new, polished, commercial kind of coffeepot, the kind you can be proud of.

The secret to his eventual success, pastor Hood goes on to note, was "starting small to do a few things and do them well."

What small things need to be grappled with in your implementation process? Where are the cold pews and faulty pots that need to be remedied? What quick wins can keep the change ball rolling?

## Quality Is Job One

Pastor T. Mac Hood's coffeepot was not just any coffeepot, but "a nice, new, polished, commercial kind of coffeepot, the kind you can be proud of." There is a connection between movement in a change process and the quality of that process. Shoddy, half-hearted, second-best improvement does little to motivate people toward innovation. However, well-done, skilled, carefully crafted improvement inspires them toward the new.

The Dickerson Church evangelism committee became sensitive to the gap between new attendees and established members. As a means of bridging this gap, they considered making name tags available to visitors and members alike on Sunday morning. A member of the committee reminded his colleagues of an important caveat: Whatever is done, must be done well.

"Our congregation," he went on, "is more prone to accept a new effort if it is done carefully and thoughtfully."

And so the committee proceeded with much intentionality; they ordered quality paper and plastic tag holders, arranged with a volunteer calligrapher to do the lettering of each name, and designed a tasteful board to hold the finished nametags. In addition, much thought went into a procedure to enable the nametags to be retrieved, replaced, and added to in a smooth and organized fashion. Though an emphasis on quality did not eliminate all aspects of awkwardness related to the name-tag effort, it did take the edge off of a new, somewhat threatening idea.

Expressions of quality vary from church to church. The following characteristics, however, appear to be basic to most settings.

## Authentic Quality Is Formed Out of Intentionality

Quality is not accidental; it is on purpose. Excellence is realized as persons strive to do highly effective worship, superior church-school teaching, and outstanding community service. Quality occurs as people make up their minds that it will occur. It takes place as individuals yearn to achieve a higher level of achievement and accomplishment.

## Authentic Quality Is Shaped by Best Efforts

Quality is attained as people contribute their best efforts. Instead of contributing leftover energy, leftover time, leftover resources, leftover furniture, and leftover ideas, people committed to quality set aside their finest efforts for Christ and Christ's church. They recognize that their best offerings are needed as congregations are nurtured and the kingdom of God expanded.

## Authentic Quality Is Developed to Bless and Serve

Quality is ultimately an expression of service and noble assistance. Excellence is not sought for self-aggrandizement, but to genuinely empower and bless another person or group.

The Benedictine monks are legendary for their high measure of service and hospitality. For decades, they would never turn away any stranger who knocked at their door; they offered choice food and lodging freely. After a time, however, their gracious gifts were abused and misused by those without legitimate need. The Benedictines determined to administer the following test: Any traveler who would allow his or her feet to be washed would be granted the hospitality of the house.

Quality, in its most brilliant, expressive form, washes the feet of others. It is the warm, sparkling water and costly perfumed ointment that soothes the cares of weary travelers and, in turn, a weary world.

# Telegraphing a Clear Message

Managing change, in large measure, is a matter of managing perception. How people view a new initiative often determines their attitude and level of support. Taking steps to communicate a clear message is a critical part of implementing change.

Sending accurate messages, however, is no easy matter. Leonard Sweet tells of a "snowbird" from the North who attempted to locate a campground with adequate toilet facilities. Too embarrassed to write the word *toilet* in her correspondence, she abbreviated her request, asking if the campground had its own "BC" (bathroom commode). Receiving the woman's letter, a campground owner passed it around, baffled by the abbreviation BC.

Finally, someone said, "Oh, that's simple. 'BC' means 'Baptist Church.' She's asking whether the campground has its own Baptist Church." So the campground owner sat down and wrote the following letter:

> Dear Madam, I'm sorry about the delay in answering your letter, but I am pleased to inform you that a BC is located just nine miles north of the campground. The last time my wife and I went was six years ago. I would like to say it pains me greatly not to be able to go more regularly, but it is surely no lack of desire on my part. As we grow older, it seems to be more of an effort, especially in cold weather. If you decide to come to our campground, perhaps I could go with you the first time. Remember that this is a friendly community.[7]

Communication is often a tangled web of misconception and misperception. Here are a few suggestions, then, for communicating intelligible and correct messages in your implementation process:

## *Practice Redundancy*

People seldom get a message the first time around; normally, you need to tell folks over and over again. As early as 1885, the German psychologist Hermann Ebbinghaus discovered three key truths about retention: People generally forget half of what they learn within half a day; forgetting is most rapid immediately after learning, then it levels off; thus—the more repetition, the better.[8]

In the spring of 1996, the musical *Showboat* came to the Auditorium Theater in Chicago. Coming straight off Broadway, it was destined to be a smash hit. The event's promoters, however, took no chances, beginning mass advertising for the musical in the *spring of 1995*. Over and over and over again—for many months—consumers in the greater Chicago area received a positive, upbeat message about a new entry in the cultural lineup of their community.

Apply the same principle toward your efforts for change. Echo over and over again a positive, confident message about any new entry in the spiritual lineup of the faith community. Keep telegraphing an informative, sensitive, upbeat message about the developing change effort. Lift up its benefits; herald its merits. Say over and over and over again why it's happening, and why it's worth the effort.

## Utilize the Ordinary

As you repeat your message, do so through as many "ordinary" channels and outlets as possible. For example:

*1. The Church Newsletter.* Include a regular column about a major change effort, and at least a paragraph or two for less comprehensive initiatives. Remember: What people aren't up on, they will be down on. Keep people briefed, and briefed well, through their accustomed information sources.

Be creative in your approach. One communication-savvy church prints the name and date of an especially important congregational event on newsletter mailing labels, above the name and address of the recipient. The event stands out because of its prominence in such an unusual location.

Another creative church utilizes a regular column by the Church Mouse. Written in a whimsical, upbeat fashion, the column addresses various congregational issues—some awkward and controversial. For example, one week the Church Mouse responded to complaints regarding the temperature setting in the sanctuary:

> RE: Too "cool" and too "hot" in the sanctuary. We try to set [the temperature] where we believe most people will be comfortable. For those of you who find it "too cool," may I suggest that you try changing your seat and bring along a wrap. For those of you who find it "too hot"—try changing your seat and dress in lighter-weight clothing. I, myself, am running around so much that I don't notice. We'll try our best to keep you comfortable![9]

Use of a whimsical voice such as the Church Mouse can communicate a volume of information in an entertaining yet effective fashion.

*2. Bulletins and Bulletin Inserts.* Along with the church newsletter, the worship bulletin is a steady, influential channel of communication. People carefully scan the information found there to pick up the pulsebeat of their congregation. It is striking how much even a few lines of bulletin copy (like attendance or offering counts) affect a person's perception.

Harry Emerson Fosdick altered the philanthropy pattern of Riverside Church in New York by placing six simple words in his worship bulletin on a weekly basis: "Remember the church in your will." Include in your bulletin a few words aimed at undergirding and reinforcing the message of your newest project or ministry endeavor.

For major change efforts, carefully produced bulletin inserts can be helpful as well. If used selectively and designed with strong graphic appeal, bulletin inserts pack a big punch, adding impact and stature to your message.

*3. Bulletin Boards.* Bulletin boards still can be found on the walls of most church buildings. Most tend to be rather mediocre, however, with little eye appeal. Imagine, then, the impact if you transform a typical church bulletin board into a colorful message center for the new adult Sunday school class, the recently developed food pantry, or the new evangelism outreach. When people walk by, they will take notice.

### Utilize the Unusual

As you repeat your message, do so through as many unusual channels and outlets as possible. For example:

*1. Skits.* Drama is a powerful and captivating communication tool. It is attractive for a number of reasons, including its versatility. Drama can employ solo performers or groups. It can be performed with props and scenery, or with no staging. It can utilize professionally produced scripts, homegrown scripts, or no scripts at all. It can communicate with spirited dialogue, or with profound, mimed silence.

Whatever method or form of drama you employ must be done well. A poorly done skit can offend people, pulling them away from a new ministry effort; a carefully enacted skit, however, can disarm people, pulling them toward a new ministry effort. If you choose this path of communication, keep three pointers in mind: prepare and practice your presentation; avoid the feel of blatant advertising; include humor.

2. *Video.* Television has changed all the rules regarding communication. If efforts to get the word out do not include the animated and the visual, people tend not to listen. Given the popularity of VCRs and camcorders, practically every congregation has access to video equipment. Consider motivating your folks toward a new ministry enterprise through video.

One large membership congregation prepared video clips extolling the virtues of attending the new Saturday evening service. One clip showed a well-known lay leader playing golf on Sunday morning after attending church on Saturday evening; another clip pictured a busy family of five, driving into a clog-free church parking lot, as opposed to the crowded lots of Sunday morning; yet a third clip humorously portrayed a fresh and lively pastor at the Saturday evening service, contrasted with the same pastor, groggy and sleepy at the Sunday morning service.

Not every congregation has the energy or interest for video production. But don't be too quick to eliminate it as an option, especially as the MTV generation continues to express passion—and expertise—in this medium.

## *Tell Stories*

The ultimate communication strategy is the strategy of story. Whether one utilizes video, drama, bulletin boards, worship bulletins, or newsletters, the inclusion of story cranks up the current of communication. Few things are more compelling than a story of life-change resulting from a new ministry effort.

As Don Delany struggled to implement a Mother's Day Out program at Christ Our Servant Church, members of the congregation's Witness Commission were his fiercest critics.

"We don't want all those kids messing up our new Fellowship Hall," Chairman Harold Butterfield would often snap. Other commission members quickly chimed in, adding momentum to Butterfield's quest to shut down the program.

Determined to keep Mother's Day Out afloat, Delany scrambled for ideas. As he racked his brain, the name of Nancy Hodkins came to mind. Nancy was one of the first mothers to take advantage of the program and had been greatly helped. It was only logical, Don thought, to ask Nancy to speak during a Moment for Mission slot on Sunday morning.

Sharing from the heart, Nancy told of her routine as a single parent; not only did she care for three rambunctious preschool children, she also traveled three hours a week to support her invalid mother. It was obvious that without Mother's Day Out, Nancy would have little time for herself or the opportunity to visit her ailing parent. People were especially touched as she shared details of the tender, personal care she was able to give her mother, week after week after week. Not surprisingly, there wasn't a dry eye in the sanctuary—including Harold Butterfield's.

Stories penetrate. While facts, figures, and reason often skim the surface of overloaded lives, stories plumb the depths, shaping an awareness of what really counts.

## Mustering Momentum

Effective communication brings sustained movement, and sustained movement eventually leads to momentum—a prime goal in implementing a new idea. Momentum is largely a gift, but certain actions encourage it:

### *Cheerleading*

Sometimes a pastor or lay leader can do too much in launching a new project or ministry. Stories are common of leaders who attempt to control all aspects of a project or new ministry endeavor. Disciples of Christ pastor Kathleen Chesson sees her role not as doing everything, but as cheerleading everything. In a telephone interview, she affirmed the positive outcomes of a supportive, equipping ministry:

"Now the leadership is really building, and that is exciting," she explained. "[People] understand that they have the freedom to express themselves."[10]

Cheerleading can take any number of forms. One experienced urban pastor utilizes the telephone frequently, calling key board members and project coordinators with an encouraging word. He is careful to include no formal agenda, other than a message of care and confidence in their leadership.

A veteran rural pastor utilizes lots of handwritten notes. Not only does he write numerous notes of support himself, he advocates that his parishioners write notes as well. In the back of the sanctuary pews are encouragement cards, which worshipers have learned to fill out on a regular basis. The cards are then sent to various members in the church, solely for the purpose of support and encouragement.

In whatever fashion, cheer your people and team members on as they do the work of ministry. Stick to your implementation plan. Work through those who are designated to carry out each particular step along the way.

## *Celebrating*

Nothing impedes an implementation process like the absence of excitement. Church leaders are notorious for emphasizing the cost of discipleship at the expense of the joy of discipleship. Yet joy is at the heart of the gospel. Numerous parties mark the New Testament, from the wedding at Cana to the reception afforded the prodigal son in the course of his homecoming.

As your change plan progresses, celebrate every little victory you can. When the new keyboard arrives, arrange for a festive dedication service; when the new senior-citizens group is organized, give all participants a colorful T-shirt marking the occasion; on the first anniversary of the new family-life center, order a cake and have a party. Look for ways to bring zest and zeal to your new ministries.

Christine Oscar, pastor of St. Mary's Church in Greensboro, North Carolina, tells of the time her four-year-old niece, Alisha, celebrated communion with her lunch:

> She seemed to have memorized the words of institution quite well, except when it came to the cup. She was heard to say, "And Jesus took the cup, and he blessed it, and he gave God thanks for it, and he said, 'Fill it with Folgers and wake 'em up!'"[11]

An effective implementation process wakes up a change effort, launching it beyond mere dreams and visions toward a celebration of God's new reality.

# CHAPTER 9

# GRAPPLING WITH RESISTANCE

## PRINCIPLE: REDUCE, RATHER THAN RESIST RESISTANCE

Not surprisingly, the seminar room was filled. The announced topic was a hot one: Managing Change. Pencils and notebooks in hand, seminar participants expected the lecturer to begin spinning out the latest theories on innovation and change. He did nothing of the kind. Instead, he walked seminar participants through a series of exercises. For starters, he asked the group to cross their arms, then to cross them the other way.

"How did that feel?" he asked. Then he asked them to write their name, first with their favored hand, then with the other.

"How did that feel?" he once again quizzed the group.

By now the people were not only curious but slightly agitated. Finally, the seminar lecturer asked the participants sitting at the end of each row to stand, turn their chairs, and face the other way. Reluctantly, and with some resistance, they stood and followed his instructions. The seminar continued. The longer the leader talked, the higher the anxiety level rose.

Finally a participant broke in: "Can you tell us what all this is about?"

"I thought you would never ask," the leader responded. "This seminar isn't only about managing change, it's about feeling change as well." And so the group began to debrief, sharing the awkwardness and frustration of moving out of their accustomed routine.

Given the awkwardness and frustration of change, is it any wonder that people resist? In similar circumstances, we would do the same. The secret of reckoning with resistance is to expect it. Rather than being dismayed or rattled by opposition to change, we are called to understand it, working with people to minimize its disruption.

## *PRINCIPLE: REDUCE, RATHER THAN RESIST RESISTANCE*

More than 400 pastors were asked to say yes or no to the following statement: "In general, it is better to work carefully and minimize resistance to change rather than 'resisting the resistance' so hard that conflict situations result." Over 81 percent of respondents answered in the affirmative.[1]

In reality, any other approach escalates feelings of alienation, resentment, and hostility. Oak Lawn Church was a declining congregation in the Pacific Northwest. In its twenty-fifth year, the congregation seriously began to consider moving to a new location. The resulting discussion revealed positions sharply divided, along lines of age and length of membership. Older, long-term members of the congregation expressed deep attachment to the existing building and location. Younger, newer members expressed excitement about a new building in an area of rapid community growth.

In the ensuing discussion, the senior pastor sided openly with the younger members; in addition, he showed impatience with the older members. Several persons in this latter category felt personally attacked from the pulpit for resisting the move. As the conflict escalated, older members withdrew their budget support, forcing a cancellation of building plans. Several younger members subsequently dropped their membership.

Railing against opposition too strongly can escalate differences of opinion into a full-scale conflict. While a lowering of emotional temperatures is not a cure-all, it does encourage people to interact more sanely and wisely. To fiercely combat resistance results in someone being a loser, a devastating category that stirs up the worst in each of us. A sermon title penned by preacher Ernest Campbell summarizes well the inevitable consequence of such behavior: "I Win, We Lose."

# Think Win-Win

Some congregations have found a consensus style of decision making—as opposed to a more competitive style—to be a helpful strategy in minimizing resistance. Though not always possible or advisable, a consensus style of moving ahead can pay rich dividends of trust, ownership, and goodwill.

Consensus building is more than milk-toast acquiescence. One church leader put it this way:

> It isn't just a matter of the majority waiting around until the minority reluctantly agree that they'll help with the project. It's founded on mutual respect. When there is a clear difference of opinion, people simply keep talking and comparing ideas and trying to understand each other. That may result in the majority making a change—deciding they shouldn't move ahead, since the minority can't be persuaded that it's right. Or it may result in the minority deciding that the decision is one they should support, even though it may not reflect their preference.[2]

As a general rule, consensus decision making works most effectively in small to medium-sized settings. The larger the group or organization, the more difficult to obtain unanimity. But a spirit of consensus can permeate any decision-making process, if you follow two guidelines: (1) Saturate your decision-making process with mutual respect;. (2) Postpone any vote or decision until a significant majority  are accepting of the new direction.

Factored into a consensus style is the emotional price tag of a particular issue. This is assessed by weighing the value of both the decision itself and the investment of various members. One Louisiana congregation, for example, engaged in a heated debate over a change of location for Sunday school classes. The Christian Education commission, which originally proposed the change, failed to anticipate a firestorm of criticism both from older-adult classes (which had met in the same rooms for years) and from teachers of children's classes (who had invested time and money in painting and decorating classrooms).

While the logic of the proposed changes was clear to the Christian Education commission, the emotional price tag of moving ahead was greater than the value of the changes. The commission wisely decided to delay action. More involvement and consensus from classes and leaders was needed.

However, there are moments, legitimate moments, when leaders simply need to lead. The vote must be taken and the chips must fall where they will. But count well the cost. With chips come sparks, and with sparks, fire, which becomes deadly if not managed and contained. Wisely steward your energy, picking your battles with much godly discernment.

## What Is Your Effectiveness Factor?

Moving toward change in the face of resistance depends upon intuition and timing. When events and people feel off-target, we slow down the change process; when things begin to fall together, we speed up the process, perhaps even pushing for resolution.

Along with intuition, one also might use some form of mathematical equation to establish a sense of timing and right movement. Knox Talbert developed one such formula out of his experience pastoring in the Dallas, Texas, area.[3] His approach is practical and applicable to most change endeavors:

1. Identify the change that needs to be made.
2. Rank that change on a scale from 1 to 10, with 10 representing major innovation.
3. Identify your resistance. How many people and groups are opposing? Though you do not want to minimize your critics, neither do you want to magnify them.

The story is told of a farmer who came to town and asked a restaurant owner if he could use a million frog legs. The owner asked where he could find so many frogs.

"I've got a pond at home just full of them," the farmer answered. "They drive me crazy night and day."

After the restaurant owner and the farmer settled for several hundred frogs, the farmer went back to his property.

Two weeks later, he approached the restaurant proprietor with two scrawny frogs and an embarrassed look on his face.

"I guess I was wrong," he stammered. "There were just two frogs in the pond, but they sure were making a lot of noise!"

4. Don't magnify your opposition! Rank your resistance on a scale from 1 to 10, with 10 representing major opposition.
5. Determine your effectiveness factor by multiplying your resistance rank by your change rank, then subtracting the total from 100 percent. For example, if the proposed innovation is changing the name of your congregation, that would probably rank a 10. Let's say that resistance is fairly high, at an 8. Your effectiveness factor would be 20 percent.

Though not an exact science, Knox Talbert's formula can help you determine when to slow or speed up a change process. If you can muster only an effectiveness factor of 20 percent, for example, it is probably not the best time to change the name of the congregation. Wise leaders pull back the throttle of change when they sight signs of probable failure; foolish leaders push the stick forward, barreling ahead at any expense.

## No Surprises, Please

Whether you pull back the throttle or push ahead, let people know—in advance—what's coming. Like a railroad signal and routing system, we need to let people and groups know—before the fact—what tracks will be employed, what equipment is engaged, and what schedule and time-table is being utilized.

One of the primary catalysts for resistance is the element of surprise. Reflecting on her attempts to change congregational worship, Priscilla Eppinger-Mendes, an American Baptist pastor, notes:

[Changes] have been much better received when I have gone through a process and not just surprised people—when they have been discussed by the Board of Deacons, when there has been some explanation of "What is the purpose of this?" "What are we trying to accomplish or achieve?" . . . To do something without anyone else knowing about it ahead of time has really been counterproductive and caused myself, as well as a lot of other people, a lot of grief.[4]

At least four antidotes to surprise stand out in Eppinger-Mendes' experience: (1) labor in advance; (2) determine who needs to be with you and for you; (3) work the system, don't circumvent it; (4) explain everything.

Minimizing surprises requires great discipline on the part of the leader. It necessitates forethought: move mentally four or five steps ahead of your people, anticipate needed next moves. As we affirmed in chapter 1, effective leaders set aside up to twenty percent of their time for personal reflection and strategizing. Some leaders accomplish this through a regular once-a-quarter planning day, to ponder possible next steps; others utilize their driving time for creative thinking and forethought; still others brainstorm with a trusted colleague or coworker on a routine basis, testing ideas and possible scenarios for action.

Choose the style that works best for you, and block out regular periods for deliberate planning and strategizing. Unless you leave time for creative pondering and anticipation, you may find yourself making last-minute dashes to judgment, leaving your people surprised, startled, and resistant.

## Different Strokes for Different Folks

Along with general preferences—like a preference for not being surprised—people also have specific preferences in the midst of a change process. Ignoring these preferences can lead to significant resistance.

Numerous typologies profile the personality styles or temperaments of persons. Two of the best known are the Myers-Briggs Type Indicator and the Personal Profile or DISC Profile.[5] Because it is unrealistic in most cases to have an entire congregation, or even a committee take this kind of testing, consider a simpler typology.

As you think of your congregation, think of people in one of four disposition categories: eagles, peacocks, owls, and sparrows.[6] What follows is a profile of each personality type, a listing of what "ruffles their feathers," and a remedy for resistance.

### Eagles

These are the "type A" folks in your midst. They push hard toward objectives and soar high to achieve. *Motto:* "Winning isn't everything; it's the only thing!" *Ruffled by:* A slow or impeded process, along with confusion regarding their piece of the action. *Remedy:* Expedite the process whenever possible, giving eagles key leadership roles and room to fly.

### Peacocks

These are the outgoing, colorful types in your fellowship. They tend to go with the flow, are easily adaptable and highly relational. *Motto:* "Don't worry; be happy." *Ruffled by:* The absence of fun and apparent pay-off from the process. *Remedy:* Build regular times of celebration into the process, emphasizing the benefits of the new event or ministry through one-on-one encounters.

### Owls

These are the contemplatives and thinkers in the group. They tend to be rather serious about life, concerned with philosophical underpinnings. *Motto:* "Plan your work and work your plan." *Ruffled by:* Confusion regarding the "reason why," along with uncertainty concerning the details of a particular action. *Remedy:* Lift up and underscore the reason why, along with providing lots of inside information.

### Sparrows

These are the behind-the-scenes folks in your fellowship. They tend to be industrious, but lack initiative and leadership skill. *Motto:* "Where you lead, I will follow." *Ruffled by:* A lack of clear, explicit guidance. *Remedy:* Provide clear instructions, along with lots of encouragement, reassurance, and inclusion.

Though all analogies break down at a certain point, these four temperament categories give some means of navigating the currents of resistance. Beyond any specific classification, however, is this truth: people resist change for different reasons, out of the differences deep within their disposition and personhood. Managing resistance is not just a generalized activity, but one with specificity, geared toward the distinct needs of distinct people.

## Keep Close to Your Enemies

In *Godfather II*, Michael Corleone travels back to his old stomping ground in New York City. As he sits in his boyhood home, a friend asks him how he intends to tackle all his problems.

Michael responds: "Pop taught me many lessons in this house. One of them was to keep your friends close and keep your enemies closer."[7]

Our natural tendency is to back away from our critics. Church leaders tend to have a passion to please; encountering persons who are not pleased is taxing relationally and emotionally. We find it much easier to avoid such individuals and move on with life. Nevertheless, the wise leader engages critics with candor and civility.

### Seek People Out

Don't wait for critics to come to you; rather, go to your critics. See your antagonists by appointment. Pick a place where both of you will feel safe.

Reaching out to critics requires courage on the part of change agents; it is never easy to take the first step. Critics know this and, in most cases, are secretly impressed. The very fact that you take the initiative softens the ground of resistance, laying a foundation for relational development.

### Be Vulnerable

As you confront your critics, confess that their criticism stings. People are not always aware of how hurtful their words can be. Also confess that you are eager to find common ground.

Vulnerability catches even the fiercest critic off guard. Defensiveness and debate is agitating, but revelation and exposure is disarming.

### Don't Argue

Critics often raise issues that will turn up the temperature in your conversation. Resist the temptation to become argumentative.

Pastor Jenny Jackson-Adams observes, "The harder you work at trying to convince these people, the more energy they are going to put into redoubling their efforts to prove you can't do that, and so you find yourself going in circles. They are into power many times, and they think you are just trying to control them."[8]

### Ask Their Advice

Instead of arguing, share the challenge of carrying out the new ministry in question. Go into some detail. Ask for the resister's counsel on a particular part of your implementation process. Talk about constructive, positive steps. Value their opinion.

Soliciting the counsel and advice of others turns the tables in even distant, strained relationships.

### Invite Their Participation

Offer a specific opportunity for critics to bring their opinion to bear on the new ministry endeavor. Show personal interest in the contribution they can bring to the project.

Name a number of strategic trigger points, where the critic could make a decisive difference. Avoid naming token or minimal contributions; stress the pivotal nature of their possible involvement and how they could be of significant influence. Stress the unique and special role they could play.

### Give Them Space

A famed Japanese artist displayed a large painting. In the far left corner was a tree, with a number of tiny birds huddled on a limb. The rest of the canvas was empty.

When the artist was asked if he intended to paint anything more in the blank space, he said, "Oh, no. I have to leave room for the birds to fly."

So too for us in our encounters with critics. We need to leave room for them to fly. Don't push. Give resisters the room to make up their own minds, in their own time. Allow space for the embryo of life-change to develop and take wing.

## The Geometry of Opposition

Even if we engage our critics with maturity and grace, we still may be seduced by the immaturity of others. This often occurs as we participate in gossip or negative conversation about critical, resistant people.

Imagine that Chalmer Quigley, chair of the Property and Finance Commission, approaches you about the new church-sign project. The first part of Chalmer's comments are on target, as he discusses the proposed dimensions of the sign and the two bids received from manufacturing companies.

But then Quigley turns the conversation toward Rosco Mattingly, a member of the congregation's Evangelism Committee. Rosco is against the proposed sign because it doesn't include adjustable space for advertising ministry events. Chalmer Quigley is vicious as he trashes Mattingly for his opposition to the project.

While not being a member of the Rosco Mattingly fan club yourself, you join in making a few cutting remarks. Rationalizing your attack, you think, "Well, I've got to ventilate my frustration some place."

This kind of encounter is referred to as an emotional triangle, a relational threesome formed by two hostile persons and a sympathetic third party. In the case of the hypothetical situation described above, Chalmer and Rosco are the hostile persons, while you are the sympathetic third party. The basic law of emotional triangles is this: In order for Chalmer to keep bashing Rosco, Chalmer needs someone to validate him. Such validation occurs when either leaders or followers sympathetically join the bashing.

Perpetuating a spirit of criticism, however, does little to reduce resistance in a congregation. Leaders are called to avoid being triangled. We do so by containing our own anxiety, rather than ventilating it to congregational members. Such a leader becomes a calming influence. From Edwin Friedman's perspective, church leaders' ability "to contain their own anxiety regarding congregational matters, both those not related to them, as well as those where they become the identified focus, may be the most important significant capability in their arsenal."[9]

Don't underestimate the importance of a calming, tranquil, non-anxious influence. When a congregational system is nervous, anxious, and resistant, it is amazing to see the impact of leadership that is steady, centered, and open.

## Take It to the Church

But what if one-on-one encounters with critics and efforts to de-triangle fail? What if resistance escalates? The practical teaching of Matthew 18 provides an avenue of escape. After talking and dealing with persons individually, the change agent has the option of involving others (see Matt. 18:16-17).

Indiana pastor Kurt Snyder has found himself in this kind of scenario.

In a telephone interview, he described his approach to church leadership:

> I take [the resistant people or problem] to my leadership, and I say, "Here is what we are doing. Is it consistent with the vision the congregation has called out? Is it consistent with scripture? Am I missing it somewhere?" And if the answer to all of those is affirmative, then I say, "Let's decide how we are going to deal with some people in your congregation." I try to make sure they see that the leadership, whether it is the deacons or the board . . . are the ones responsible for the ministry of this church."[10]

Snyder's counsel is sound and strategic: Don't try to go it alone. Avoiding triangles is not to be confused with avoiding support. At key bends in the resistance river, seek help in navigating the obstacles before you. Second, make clear who's ultimately responsible.

Snyder points out, "If the statistics prove out, I might die here, but I also might leave in the next six months or three years. They [the lay leadership] are the ones responsible for dealing with the people who live and worship here."

Don't over-function as a leader. Setting limits and boundaries on our efforts to negotiate resistance is vital—not only for your own health, but for the health of your congregation as well.

## CAPs

Some people are never satisfied. John Yates tells of a young man standing in a post office. Approached by an older gentleman, the lad was asked to address a postcard. Obliging, he addressed the card, wrote a short message per the senior's instruction, and even signed the man's name.

With a sense of satisfaction, the lad turned to the elderly man and asked, "Is there any other way I can serve you?"

The senior thought for a moment, looking at his completed postcard. "Yes, at the end could you just put, 'P.S. Please excuse the sloppy hand-writing.'"[11]

Chronically dissatisfied folks certainly include the ungrateful. But they also include a subcategory of obstructive people, bluntly described through yet another bird analogy—vultures. These are brutal persons who thrive on tearing apart new ideas, projects, ministries, and even people. Most congregations have at least one person in this category. Peter Steinke types such individuals in a clinical fashion–Chronically **A**nxious **P**eople (CAPs):

> [Such persons] are apt to conduct a "search and destroy mission." . . . Basically, chronically anxious people have a low threshold for pain. This is why they are in the forefront of the effort to secure immediate relief. . . . Threatened, they make demands, spread rumors, exaggerate circumstances, claim injustice—whatever it takes to lessen their anxiety. Governed by instinct rather than insight, they cannot be stopped by reasoning or appeasing.[12]

As you deal with chronically anxious people (CAPs), try these four approaches:
1. Own the fact that CAPs cannot be stopped by reason or appeasement.
2. In partnership with other leaders, formulate strategies for restraining CAP behavior.
3. Factor CAPs out of your support system. Don't expect such people to want you, like you, or even respect you.
4. Keep your distance. Detach yourself from CAPs without divorcing.

Given our longing to be liked, we might be tempted to relentlessly pursue CAPs. But beware: Their sickness can become our sickness. Avoid becoming enmeshed in their neurotic behavior.

## The Up Side of Resistance

A certain amount of conflict is healthy in a church, and one shouldn't be bothered when resistance to change creates conflict. Surprisingly, over 70 percent of church leaders express agreement with this statement when polled by the Change and the Established Congregation Project.[13] But how can the presence of opposition and conflict be viewed as *healthy* reality? From a redemptive perspective, what can resistance represent? Among other things, it signals that:
1. People are actively, not passively, engaged in the change process.
2. Authentic community is taking place, as feelings surface, rather than being stuffed.

3. The church is exercising its prophetic role, taking risks and challenging the status quo.

These affirmations are not intended to put a Band-Aid on the genuine misery, heartache, and sleepless nights that resistance often causes. Nor are they a rationalization to give CAPs free reign; that would be tragic. Rather, these statements clarify and affirm that in every situation of life, there is both a downside and an upside to the reality that God allows.

Warren Bennis states: "Everywhere you trip is where the treasure lies."[14] It is in adversity that advances are often realized. It is the strained muscle that develops; it is the challenged mind that reaches new understanding; it is the striving, often stressed congregation that travels to new heights of growth and faithfulness.

# CHAPTER 10

# BOLSTERING
# BOLD BEGINNINGS

## PRINCIPLE: TAKE STEPS TO SOLIDIFY
## YOUR NEW BEGINNING

Millard Fuller frequently tells stories to illustrate the remarkable witness made by his organization, Habitat for Humanity. One of his favorites concerns Habitat's experience in south Florida during hurricane Andrew. In more than one location, the only houses left standing after the storm were those built by Habitat for Humanity volunteers. Startled by this phenomena, the news media quizzed Fuller for an explanation.

"For starters," Fuller would begin, "these houses aren't just built out of wood and shingles; these houses are built out of love."

Pressed for further explanation, Fuller would add, "And with the love is the factor of prayer. There is an awful lot of prayer going into these homes."

Pressed even further, Fuller would relent and give a practical explanation:

> Well, if you want me to be perfectly honest, these homes are really built. I mean *really* built! You see, most of our Habitat volunteers actually don't know what they are doing. And so, if the specs call for one two-by-four, they might just put in two. And if the specs call for three nails, I guarantee you they put in seven. They reinforce things, just for the peace of mind.[1]

Wise change agents do the same: They reinforce things, just for the peace of mind. For the storms will pound and the resistance will come. A successful change launch requires ongoing bracing, bolstering, and buttressing.

## PRINCIPLE: TAKE STEPS TO SOLIDIFY YOUR NEW BEGINNING

# Multiplying Ownership

One of the most important ways to bolster and solidify a new project or ministry is to expand ownership. Change efforts can withstand opposition when a growing number of people cast their lot with the new effort.

Industrialist Andrew Carnegie referred to this phenomenon as the formation of strategic coalitions or alliances. Like rods of iron wrapped one around the other, strategic coalitions form incredibly strong cables of change, capable of pulling a congregation effectively into the future.

Not expanding ownership, of course, results in regression. One pastor worked for months to convince her music committee to change the number of hymns in the order of worship from four to five. After hours of skillful negotiation, she finally had the support and ownership of the committee. Expectantly, the pastor looked forward to the first Sunday when the new order of worship would be used. The service went exceptionally well until the very end; the organist walked out on the fifth hymn.

To avoid a walkout in your congregation, consider these practical pointers for deepening ownership in a change effort.

## *Secure Cosponsors*

As a general rule, resist sponsoring new events alone. Whenever possible, cosponsor activities with another group or individual in the congregation. For example, rather than continuing to solo sponsor the new outreach to homeless men, the Social Action Committee would be wise to bring the Men's Fellowship on board as joint sponsor.

Cosponsorship of a new effort casts a powerful message to a congregation. Individual efforts always seem to be suspect, conjuring up images of "empire building," self-aggrandizement, or political advancement. Team efforts, however, encourage images of servanthood, mutual aid, and shared power.

Bethany Church, a growing congregation in Southern California, added its first minister of music to its staff. Some senior members worried about how the music in the church might change. But the minister of music wisely designed a Christmas musical to be performed by both the Sunday school children and the Senior Citizens' choir. The older members, rather than feeling displaced, felt a sense of pride and ownership in the new musical. Both seniors and children gained a new appreciation for those with whom they rehearsed and performed.

As you think of cosponsors, think of individuals or groups with which you have some affinity. Sharing a common vision and chemistry does much to facilitate a partnership effort. Also think of individuals or groups that have significant standing in your congregation. Though you want to avoid being blatantly political, an eye toward people and groups of influence can produce effective coalitions.

### Share the Limelight

President Ronald Reagan kept a bronze plaque on his desk: "There is no limit to what a man can accomplish if he doesn't care who gets the credit." Nothing deadens ownership like an individual or group that grabs recognition.

Paul Minnich Robinson was a noted seminary educator in the Chicago area for many years. Prior to his academic career, Robinson was pastor of the largest Church of the Brethren congregation in the United States. Over a thirteen-year period, he skillfully developed that congregation into a strong and vibrant fellowship. In interviewing persons regarding Robinson's effectiveness, one theme recurs: "Paul Robinson had a knack for letting his ideas become your ideas." Robinson didn't monopolize the limelight. He worked through people, implementing vision through shared power and influence.

Where do you need to mete out power and influence? Where do you or other leaders need to share the limelight?

### Seek Outside Validation

We've looked at the role of legitimizers from within a congregation. The wise leader will connect also with legitimizers from outside the congregation. People own the new when persons in authority have legitimized it. For instance, as you develop an after-school program, people will own the new effort more readily if they know that the program will use a reputable outside curriculum or program kit. Why? Because more than your reputation is in the picture; Pioneer Clubs, Inc., or Venture Clubs, Inc., or Youth Clubs, Inc., or Awana Clubs, Inc. have shared their good name as well. It is akin to having a Good Housekeeping Seal of Approval affixed to your ministry. People own what they trust.

Other examples of outside stamps of approval include a noted community leader's endorsement of your new youth basketball outreach program; a judicatory executive's blessing on your plans to expand facilities and shoulder new debt; a college president's applause for your intent to establish a scholarship fund for those attending church-related institutions of higher education; a consultant's guidance in designing an outreach emphasis.

Hitch your wagon to a star. Ride the coattails of credible people. Seek out the endorsements of those who already have been endorsed.

## Midcourse Corrections

Change efforts are bolstered and solidified, not only through multiplying ownership, but also through midcourse correction. At one time, it was possible to plan accurately five or more years into the future; today organizational consultants advise plans of no more than two to three years.

Even the most successful change launch is doomed without a commitment to ongoing monitoring and midcourse modification. A commitment to midcourse modification requires both awareness and humility.

### *Awareness*

Many congregations have no system of feedback and evaluation, other than the proverbial grapevine. Making midcourse corrections is difficult if you have no awareness of how you are doing.

The business world has long recognized the indispensable role of feedback and evaluation. Boston Market, for example, has established an automated feedback survey accessed through a special toll-free number. Customers are enticed to call the number through special "Feedbucks" coupons that can be redeemed only by writing in a code word supplied by the automated survey.

Though automated surveys and "Feedbucks" are not in the realm of possibility for most churches, some feedback mechanism can be established as a part of congregational life. Generally, the simpler the better. Many congregations have found the use of "I Wish" cards to be helpful. Available from most church supply stores, these cards guide the respondent through a series of "I Wish" options ("I Wish to Speak to the Pastor"; "I Wish Our Church Would . . . ," etc., with a blank option that can be personalized).

Other congregations have found the establishment of a suggestion box or the inclusion of a simple index card in the worship bulletin to be a fruitful feedback source—especially for special issues or concerns. One staff member of a rural large-membership church uses what he calls the Ed Koch approach. Like the famed mayor of New York City, this man routinely moves through the congregation, asking, "How am I doing?" Many parishes simply use an evaluation form after events and meetings, along with formal program evaluation sessions, often facilitated by a judicatory executive.

In addition to these options, each of the strategies listed in chapter 6 for initially involving others—mini-surveys, cottage meetings, and listening sessions—also can be utilized for involving others in an ongoing cycle of response. In whatever way, find a way to keep abreast of what's working and what's not.

## Humility

As we receive feedback, it will, in all probability, contain some evidence of mistakes and misjudgment. Not everything works in a new ministry endeavor. This is painful and humbling for most of us; we hold to the illusion that vision can be implemented without error. Of all people, however, the people of God should be aware of the reality of human fragility and the inevitability of human error.

When directly posed with the option of admitting error, most people do feel that it is the best recourse. When asked whether it is important to be honest with people when changes in the church do not produce the desired result, over 94 percent of church leaders answer in the affirmative.

In some respects, the marketplace is ahead of the church in acknowledging the reality and role of error. Personnel directors often ask a candidate whether he or she has made any mistakes in past performance. If the answer is "No," the candidate is often passed over. If you're not making many mistakes, marketplace recruiters reason, you're probably not taking enough risks.

In a telephone interview, Mark Miller-McLemore described a series of risks taken by leadership in his northern Illinois parish. Most involved rearranging the events of Sunday morning, such as worship flow and the location of the coffee/fellowship hour. Such risk-taking involved lots of trial and error, but resulted in a strengthening of trust. He explains:

> We let failures happen along the way so that people would understand . . . that these things were not going to be rammed down their throats [at any cost]. We established a history of experimenting and being willing to lose on smaller things, yet building toward bigger things–in particular, building toward a major decision about our church's calling. People were able to buy into that process, and it really built trust.[2]

United Methodist pastor Martha Matteson describes this same process in yet another fashion:

> One of my best theories is "W.W.," which is "Whatever Works." In every ministry, you try one thing, and if it doesn't work, you try another, and say, "Well . . . I know one thing that doesn't work."[3]

Management consultant Price Pritchett underscores Matteson's train of thought:

> Inertia is more crippling than mistakes. . . . Inaction is the most costly error. . . . Just keep moving. When you foul up, fix it. Learn from your mistake and plow on. This is how you energize your organization and build momentum.[4]

When we fail, we are called to fail fast and fall forward. Make your midcourse corrections quickly, positively, and in good humor. Such leadership style bolsters a change initiative, as it adds momentum and credibility to renewal efforts.

## Tenacious Tenure

Changes that last usually are accompanied by leadership that lasts. Pastoral and lay leaders who hang in for the long haul often bring strength and fortitude to new ministry initiatives. On the other hand, leaders who prematurely leave a project or parish often damage new ministry initiatives.

## *Tenure*

Researcher George Barna has observed that over the last two decades, the average tenure of pastors has declined from seven years to four years.[5] This is quite disturbing, if you accept the premise that part of the pastoral job description is the role of missionary. It is difficult to fathom how a missionary can be effective in only four years. It takes at least that long to learn the language, appreciate the culture, and earn the trust of those you are seeking to serve. The same holds true for pastors and lay leaders who seek to connect effectively with their people.

Fourth Presbyterian Church in Chicago has had a steady story of growth and vitality for more than fourteen decades. Many factors have contributed to this stability, including a prime location, wealth and endowment, and excellent demographics. But significant internal factors have contributed as well, one of the most prominent being impressive pastoral tenure—only three pastors during those seventy-five years.[6]

Ministry cannot be done without deep connection. Leadership in the church is essentially a relational enterprise, built on credibility, trust, and love. Nicholas Van Dyck, president of Religion in American Life, once made an interesting observation about fund-raising. Individuals normally do not give money to an organization, he commented. They give money to a person—in his case, a board member or executive leader within the organization. Though we may be reluctant to admit it, the same holds true for the church. Sheer tradition or ecclesiastical structure seldom motivates people toward major giving. Rather, it is the integrity and trustworthy track record of the leadership of the congregation that motivates people toward sacrificial sharing. Such integrity and trustworthiness is not crafted overnight.

With great enthusiasm, a young pastor took his midsized congregation through a revision of its bylaws; an entirely new church organizational structure resulted. Many felt uneasy about the changes, fearing that much would fall through the cracks because of a more simple structure. The pastor kept reassuring them, however, that he would personally see that nothing was overlooked.

In less than six months, the pastor was invited to move to a much larger urban congregation. He accepted the position, much to the dismay of those depending on his leadership during the start-up of the new structure. And sure enough, things began to fall through the cracks. Tasks such as the recruitment of Sunday school teachers and the organization of the annual Christmas program floundered. Resentment grew throughout the church.

In early fall, a new pastor arrived, filled with energy and new vision. Unfortunately, resentment had now turned to resistance. Calls for advancement and innovation were met with suspicion, not support.

Conclusion? Don't abandon the ship before it pulls out of port. For first-level or incremental change, plan on a minimum tenure of three to five years. For second-level or paradigm-shifting change, plan on a minimum tenure of eight to ten years. Leaving before these minimum tenures borders on abandonment, often resulting in serious wounds to a congregation's psyche. Trusting once, a church might not trust again.

## *Tenacity*

Along with long tenure goes a tenacious spirit. Without sheer persistence and willpower, it is next to impossible to go the distance in a change effort. Peter Drucker is right: "Some succeed because they are destined to; most succeed because they are determined to."[7]

Resignation, however, is our common lot. When the going gets tough, we usually are prone to grouse and look for the nearest exit. Leonard Sweet tells of a graduating seminary senior. Discovering a post-commencement pastoral appointment not to his liking, he complained to a fellow student.

Responding unsympathetically, his colleague patted him on the back and said, "You know, the world is a better place because Michelangelo didn't say, 'I don't do ceilings.'"

Think about it, Sweet goes on to say. The world is a better place because

Moses didn't say, "I don't do rivers." Noah didn't say, "I don't do arks." Jeremiah didn't say, "I don't do weeping." David didn't say, "I don't do giants." Peter didn't say, "I don't do Gentiles." Mary Magdalene didn't say, "I don't do feet." Paul didn't say, "I don't do letters." Jesus didn't say, "I don't do crosses."[8]

The world is a better place when we too hang in with our calling, even in the difficult and demanding passages of ministry.

The mental steelness of a marathon runner comes to mind in thinking of a tenacious outlook. Such perseverance is forged out of a disciplined life that is focused, well paced, and goal-oriented. Without similar virtues, even the shrewdest change agent will find it difficult to "hang in" with a new endeavor.

A runner's determination is shaped by the warmth of encouragement. Without support teams and cheering fans, marathon runners cannot complete the race. Neither can we. Effective leaders create adequate support systems, including some social contact outside the congregation. Given the disruptive nature of change, it is unrealistic to expect all social support to come from within your own local church. You need outside advocates.[9]

An emphasis on either tenacity or tenure is not to suggest that there are no limits to a concerted effort. We must regularly review God's call on our lives and the Spirit's leadings. In addition, we must set personal boundaries that prompt us to monitor emotional, psychological, and physical health. The presence of adversity in and of itself, however, is not sufficient reason to abdicate. Great growth often can emerge out of great pain. Our tendency is to quit too soon.

## Of Bucks and Leaders

Wally Appington was determined to begin a Men's Prayer Breakfast at Dellinger Chapel. Though the congregation had a thriving Women's Fellowship, the men had little opportunity to congregate. And so Wally took it upon himself to fill the male fellowship vacuum.

The first prayer breakfast was well attended. People praised Wally for his planning and determination. And for good reason. Wally had secured the guest speaker and special music, set up the fellowship hall, cooked the breakfast, served as emcee, and cleaned up afterward.

For the next two and one half years, Wally continued to "do" the prayer breakfast. He would always have some help cooking, setting up, and tearing down, but essentially Wally "did" the event. That is, until he had his heart attack. Incapacitated for weeks, Wally's condition steadily worsened, resulting eventually in an untimely death.

At first Joe Shoemaker and Harry Lacher pitched in and continued the breakfasts. But they kept running into obstacles. For starters, there was no church budget money available for the event. Wally had never bothered to turn in receipts to the Fellowship Commission; he just paid for the event out of his own pocket. And then there was a lack of hands to plan and execute the breakfasts. Wally never saw the need for formal organization; he just did everything himself.

Joe and Harry tried to keep things going, but they ran out of steam in six months, and the prayer breakfasts ended. Reflecting later, Harry noted, "Wally certainly served us, but in the process, he spoiled us."

What happened at Dellinger Chapel? Why did the Men's Prayer Breakfast grind to a premature halt? For at least two reasons: inadequate leader development and inadequate financial development.

## Leader Development

A new project or ministry enterprise cannot be sustained without a growing cadre of leaders. Wally's pattern is the pattern of many of us: We tend do it all ourselves. As a general rule, we should not carry on any prolonged ministry task without mentoring someone in the process.

For example, instead of repeatedly visiting parishioners in the hospital alone, choose an individual with the gift of caring, and ask him or her to come along. The well-worn formula for leadership development is still applicable: Do a task yourself; next, invite someone to watch you do the task; then watch them do the task; then let them do the task alone.

As you look for persons to mentor, keep the principle of the unlikely in mind. Often the most effective leaders are the most unlikely people, called in the midst of the most unlikely settings. For example, when the call came to Martin Luther to lead the Reformation, he was a lowly monk, sitting on the john in his monastic cell. When the call came to C. S. Lewis to be an apologist for the Christian faith, he was an unknown academic, riding in the sidecar of his brother's bike. When the call came to Clarence Jordan to form Koinonia Farms, he was a humble agrarian, growing pecans in Georgia.[10]

Who are the Martin Luthers and Clarence Jordans in your congregation? Look for unlikely people in unlikely places as you strive toward leader development.

## *Financial Development*

Along with ongoing human resources, new-ministry ventures need ongoing financial resources. Though Wally was a generous guy, he hurt the prayer breakfast, in the long run, by not establishing some source of lasting funding.

Churches have numerous options for ongoing financial support: regular offerings, endowment funds, designated gifts, sponsorship by an individual or group. An essential source of continuing financial security, however, is setting aside some amount of money in the budget of the church.

A line item in the congregational budget has a certain power. It fixes and maintains a ministry in the self-identity of a congregation. Long after vision and relevance is recalled, budget line items stay lodged in the marrow of an organization. In 1995, Henry Foster lost a heated battle to become Surgeon General of the United States. In the wake of his defeat, Senators asked an obvious but overlooked question: Why do we even have a Surgeon General? Such a question had not been asked for more than 125 years, even though the original tasks of the office had been delegated to the Veterans Administration, and the cost of the office had escalated to 1.4 million dollars.

This illustration is not meant to encourage visionless spending, but to underscore the power of establishing a new initiative in the structure and budget of an organization. As a new ministry becomes lodged in the framework and budget of a church, it takes on permanence. The specific amount of the budget line item doesn't matter; what matters is the presence of the new ministry among established ministries. Such positioning lends credibility, further legitimizing the new effort.

# What Do You Reward?

New ministry initiatives can be bolstered or hindered by the reward system of a congregation. Every local church has one. It appears, among other places, in the worship bulletin and in the church newsletter. The names and ministries highlighted there probably are those that are truly valued in the life of your congregation.

A large, declining congregation in Sarasota, Florida, was in the habit of printing names of recently deceased members in their church newsletter.

It was a fitting tribute to loyal, departed individuals. When the recently formed evangelism task team, however, asked that the names of new members be printed as well, the church publications committee balked; there simply wasn't enough room for both. Two days later, however, the chair of that same committee was overheard complaining about empty pews and the decline of the congregation.

It certainly should not be necessary to die in order to get one's name in the newsletter! While most people do not work in the church with the expectation of praise, they are enriched when it comes their way. Letting people know that new members have been received builds excitement in a congregation. Highlighting the work of Sunday school teachers encourages people to support the educational program. Recognizing choir members makes it more likely that others will share their musical gifts.

We often don't make the connection. What we reward—what we recognize—is often what results. Recognition systems will vary from congregation to congregation. In some locales, plaques and certificates are appropriate and effective; in other settings, more relational measures, such as recognition banquets and celebrative receptions communicate what is appreciated and valued. In any event, take some intentional step to acknowledge with joy the ministries and people you want at the forefront of your congregation.

## Institutionalizing the Journey

An emphasis on bolstering and solidifying a new endeavor is not to be confused with cementing that endeavor as a permanent fixture. We do want new ministries to be long-lasting, but long-lasting is not synonymous with forever. More than institutionalizing a particular change, we are called to institutionalize the journey.

The journey or lifecyle of an organization is often illustrated by a bell curve, with birth represented on one side and decline on the other. Perhaps the most helpful representation is the sigmoid, or S curve discussed in Charles Handy's book, *The Age of Paradox.*[11] The S curve is a partial bell curve, but with a sweeping curved line rising in modified fashion from its top. Handy's thesis: Before the first curve begins to decline, start a new curve.

That is why the challenge of change is ongoing. Even the best fruit in the best wagon will eventually rot, so you need to periodically upset the apple cart—and go after new apples.

A pastor struggled to interpret the cycle of change to a group of lay leaders on retreat. As the group walked on the beach, they came across a crab skittering along the sand.

"Do any of you know the life cyle of a crab?" the pastor asked.

Everyone shook their heads no.

"In order for a crab to grow," the pastor continued, "it needs to periodically discard its old shell and grow a new shell. If it doesn't, it becomes trapped in its old shell as that shell hardens and calcifies. Eventually it dies."

"There must be a parable in all this," one of the walkers chimed in.

"Yes, there is," the pastor responded. "Just as a crab needs periodically to discard its old shell and anticipate the new, so we need periodically to discard our familiar creature comforts and anticipate the new."

"And if we don't," one of the walkers interpreted, "we end up trapped, don't we?"

"Yes, that's right," the pastor affirmed. "But it needn't be that way. God's invitation to newness comes each and every day. It comes each and every day."[12]

# *EPILOGUE*

# WHEN THE DOORS WON'T OPEN

innesota pastor Craig Haberman was skeptical about change. "Frankly," he commented in a telephone interview, "Loren Mead [founder of the Alban Institute] is right. There are no easy answers, no quick answers, and in some cases there may not even be an answer."[1]

Haberman and Mead are probably on target. The change process in churches is difficult and, at points, grueling. And yes, in some cases, there may not be an answer; in some cases, the doors might not open.

## When the Congregation Is the Cause

Congregations are often the culprit when opportunities for change do not swing wide and open. When local churches persistently thwart change, there usually are two pathological reasons: the presence of destructive viruses and waning energy.

### *Destructive Viruses*

Some local churches are profoundly sick. Inflicted with one or more stubborn, systemic viruses, they vehemently resist positive, therapeutic intervention. As an outcome of such disease, they become abusive systems, chewing up pastors and lay leaders like a meat grinder. Four major signs can alert you to a virus-ridden congregation:

*1. Subversive Communication.* Rather than communicating directly, people gossip profusely. Things go underground and become covert. Members discuss problems over cups of coffee in homes, rather than at board meetings, where they might be solved.

*2. Controlling Behavior.* Rather than expressing mutual regard and respect, people use intimidation and snubbing to manipulate others. A coercive, domineering spirit reigns supreme.

*3. Punitive Conduct.* Rather than fighting fair, people shame and blame others. A bent toward punishing enemies and retaliation prevails.

*4. Irresponsible Attitudes.* Rather than demonstrating maturity and grace, people become cavalier and arrogant. A haughty, individualist style marks relationships and the conduct of business.

Every congregation has some individuals who exhibit these marks (for example, the **C**hronically **A**nxious **P**eople, CAPs, discussed in chapter 9); it is when these individuals multiply or dominate leadership that an abusive, dysfunctional ethos overshadows congregational life.

When confronted with a sick system, the wise change agent moves immediately to establish personal boundaries, avoiding enmeshment at all costs. Next he or she considers whether third-party intervention by an outside consultant or judicatory staff member is a viable possibility. Third, the change agent explores options for incremental change and ministry, including caregiving to others afflicted by the system. Fourth, he or she establishes limits to tenure and options for future employment.

Reflecting on the reality of dysfunctional congregations, a veteran pastor of forty years noted:

No, every church cannot be turned around. Some are full of emotionally crippled people. We spend far too much time trying to renew churches that can't be renewed. We should just leave them alone and start another church full of people who want to grow.[2]

## *Waning Energy*

Some congregations are plagued, not by destructive viruses, but by waning energy. An elderly New England congregation, for example, was heavily dependent upon two young families for the initiation of a children's program. The death of the wife in one family and a divorce in the other caused both families to leave the church. The elderly congregation still desired a children's ministry, but it no longer had access to sufficient energy and resourcefulness to implement change.

No matter how hard a congregation pounds on some doors, they will not open until realistic levels of energy come into view. In some instances, it is probably best to reassess ministry objectives, focusing on the needs of the current members and some achievable minor changes.

# When the Change Agent Is the Cause

When the doors won't open, congregations are often culpable, but the change agent also can be implicated. This is especially true when the change agent relentlessly ignores one or more of the ten principles outlined in this book. Not casting vision, not respecting culture, not launching well, not reducing resistance—all can block movement toward renewal and growth. In addition, elements of chemistry and giftedness need to be considered.

## *Chemistry*

Sometimes a pastor is a poor cultural match for a congregation. This often happens, for example, when the highly trained, urban-biased seminary graduate is placed in a small rural parish. Though love and genuine caring can transcend an avalanche of awkwardness, bridging two highly divergent worlds is difficult—even with a missionary mind-set. And so the pastor fails to connect with the people, and with the disconnection is a lack of substantial change.

Church and pastor also can have personality disputes. An authoritarian-style pastor can clash with a team-oriented board; an incremental-change-oriented pastor can lock horns with a "charge ahead at any cost" lay leader. Though many personality conflicts can be mediated, sometimes a parting of the ways is the best and only solution.

## *Giftedness*

Recent research is revealing that change agents have a particular temperament and giftedness. In *Pouring New Wine into Old Wineskins,* Aubrey Malphurs devotes two entire chapters to the theme of assessment, referring to both the Personal Profile (or DISC profile) and the Myers-Briggs Type Indicator as tools for determining a portrait of the effective change agent.[3]

In general, the effective steward of innovation must be a leader, rather than a manager; an initiator, rather than a spectator; a persuader, rather than a pacifier; a problem solver, rather than a fatalist.

Like the art of leadership, the art of change agentry can be learned. Thus, the creation of this book. However, if one's natural instincts favor a ministry of maintenance (as opposed to a ministry of transformation), perhaps it is best not to attempt a major change effort.


# When the Context Is the Cause

Along with the change agent and the congregation, the context of a new ministry initiative can undermine sincere, earnest efforts. Consider for example, the following.

## *Industry Relocation*

The movement of a major factory out of the ministry area of a particular congregation can wreak havoc on a new endeavor. The resulting disruption and uncertainty can wield a deadly blow to even the most carefully crafted change initiative. Leadership is dislocated as families leave the area, often suddenly and abruptly, in search of new employment.

A related phenomena is the occurrence of major labor strikes in communities dominated by one particular industry. Often movement in the social fabric of the area is paralyzed until the labor dispute is settled. It is not uncommon for congregations in such communities to find members of both management and labor sitting at the same board table. Tensions from the workplace spill over into the church, undercutting any major new initiative.

## *Community Transition*

An increase in violence and drug use in the area around a church can have a profound impact on that congregation's efforts at outreach. While important new opportunities for witness may arise, previous commitments to membership expansion and building renovation may prove impossible as members and participants feel at risk.

Changes in the infrastructure around a church's property also can prove traumatic to new ministry endeavors. A midsized congregation in the northwest suburbs of Chicago embarked on new, ambitious plans for community witness. The congregation set aside major budget amounts for ministries to the poor, a new neighborhood children's program, and an innovative youth-outreach effort.

Just as the congregation was gearing up to launch these efforts, inspectors discovered an old underground oil tank on the church property. The oil tank was still partially filled, leaking toxic fluid into the water table. The state of Illinois declared the site environmentally unsafe, requiring full removal of the old oil tank and a major cleanup of surrounding soil. Though the state government bore some of the cost of the project, the congregation had to expend tens of thousands of dollars previously unbudgeted. Needless to say, new ministries and change efforts were put on hold indefinitely.

A change in environmental safety, planned housing development, highway location, or even weather systems (for example, a natural disaster), can force alteration of existing plans, resulting in the possible collapse of new efforts.

Changes in infrastructure and context are often major factors in determining the acceleration or decline of new ministry endeavors.

# See, I Am Making All Things New

Whether the doors open or do not open, whether the congregation, the change agent, or the context is the cause, God moves life on. In either victory or failure, our Creator advances our lives—and all of creation—toward an ultimate destination of shalom: wholeness and, yes, newness, in the kingdom of God.

Catherine Marshall tells of a plane trip to Cleveland taken by her friend Marge:

*Epilogue*

As she settled into her seat, Marge noticed a strange phenomenon. On one side of the airplane a sunset suffused the entire sky with glorious color, but out of the window next to her seat, all Marge could see was a sky dark and threatening, with no sign of sunset.[4]

As Marge traveled, the presence of God reminded her of both the sunsets and the shadows in her own life:

You see [the Lord reminded her], it doesn't matter which window you look through; this plane is still going to Cleveland. So it is with your life. You have a choice. You can dwell on the gloomy picture. Or you can focus on the bright things and leave the dark, ominous situations to Me.[5]

Whether our particular change effort succeeds or fails, whether the doors open or close, the plane is still going to Cleveland. The kingdom of God advances. We approach that day when

> "Death will be no more;
> mourning and crying and pain will be no more . . . ."

And the one . . . seated on the throne [will say], "*See, I am making all things new*" (Rev. 21:4*b*-5*a*, italics added).

# *APPENDIX*

# RESEARCH METHODOLOGY

This book draws on original research gleaned as a part of the Change and the Established Congregation Project sponsored by The Andrew Center, a multidenominational resource agency. Four hundred and seven local church leaders from a variety of denominations completed lengthy questionnaires. As they responded to this research instrument, they also provided many written comments on change and the established congregation. Special acknowledgment is given to Steve Clapp for creating the questionnaire content and form, along with compiling its results.

In addition to the survey research, more than forty phone interviews were conducted, again with a wide range of church leaders across denominational lines.

Special acknowledgment is given to Tom Longnecker and Al Pownell for assistance in conducting the telephone interviews, and to Jackie Ruhl for transcribing the results. Special acknowledgment is given to Steve Clapp and Kristen Leverton for gleaning transcripts for choice stories and pertinent quotes.

The Andrew Center office staff gave invaluable assistance in completing all phases of both the survey and the telephone research. Special thanks to Barb Faga, Andrew Center Operations Supervisor, for coordinating and supervising the hundreds of details related to the research

*Appendix*

effort. Special thanks also to Karen Carlson, Andrew Center support staff, for scheduling interviews and confirming telephone appointments.

## Telephone Interview Participants and Institutional Affiliation

| *Person* | *Affiliation* |
| --- | --- |
| Eric C. Anspaugh | Castine Church of the Brethren, Arcanum, Ohio |
| Fred Bernhard | Oakland Church of the Brethren, Arcanum, Ohio |
| Richard Boyd | Central United Methodist, Milbank, S. Dak. |
| Paul W. Brubaker | Middle Creek Church of the Brethren, Ephrata, Pa. |
| Dennis Burnett | First Presbyterian, Monaca, Pa. |
| Kathleen Kline Chesson | Henson Valley Christian, Fort Washington, Md. |
| James Chronister | Cedar Grove Church of the Brethren, New Paris, Ohio |
| Robert Cueni | Country Club Christian, Kansas City, Mo. |
| Tim Deardorff | Mexico Church of the Brethren, Mexico, Ind. |
| Ernie Deyerle | Red Hill Church of the Brethren, Roanoke, Va. |
| Judith Donaldson | United Methodist Church, Carlin, Nev. |
| William Easum | 21st Century Strategies, Port Aransas, Tex. |
| Priscilla Eppinger-Mendes | First Baptist, Plymouth, Mass. |
| James S. Flora | Frederick Church of the Brethren, Frederick, Md. |
| Jim & Rinya Frisbie | Chubbuck United Methodist, Chubbuck, Idaho |
| Craig Haberman | United Methodist Mobile Ministries, Orr, Minn. |
| Gary A. Hackenberg | Shiloh United Church of Christ, Danville, Pa. |
| Paul Hanneman | Immanuel Baptist, Portland, Maine |
| Joe Harding | United Methodist, Richland, Wash. |
| Irvin R. Heishman | First Church of the Brethren, Harrisburg, Pa. |
| Jim Hodge | First Presbyterian, Bel Air, Md. |
| Jenny Jackson-Adams | Lizella United Methodist, Americus, Ga. |
| Jeff Jones | Epworth Church, Cockeysville, Md. |
| Susan Keirn Kester | Grace United Methodist, Wilmington, Del. |
| Rick Kirchoff | Christ United Methodist, Memphis, Tenn. |
| T. Mac Hood | First United Methodist, Livingston, Tex. |
| Martha D. Matteson | Pataskala United Methodist, Pataskala, Ohio |
| Bill Maylew | First Baptist, National City, Calif. |

| | |
|---|---|
| Roy Miller | Wesley United Methodist, Alexandria, Va. |
| Mark Miller-McLemore | First Christian Church, Chicago Heights, Ill. |
| James Moss, Sr. | People Spots, Harrisburg, Pa. |
| Jimmy Ross | Lititz Church of the Brethren, Lititz, Pa. |
| Erick Sawatzky | Southside Fellowship, Elkhart, Ind. |
| Norman Shawchuck | Shawchuck & Assoc., Ltd., Leith, N. Dak. |
| Richard Shreckhise | Annville Church of the Brethren, Annville, Pa. |
| Kurt Snyder | Roann Church of the Brethren, Roann, Ind. |
| John Thorington | First Christian Church, Quincy, Ill. |
| Margaret M. Twesme | St. John's Lutheran, Melrose Park, Pa. |
| Harry Vein | First United Methodist, Cleveland, Tex. |
| Jerome D. Ward | Kidder Memorial United Methodist, Jamestown, N.Y. |
| Barry W. Wehrle | Ridgewood United Methodist, Ridgewood, N.J. |
| Elaine Wilson | Wesley United Methodist, Minneapolis, Minn. |
| Earl Ziegler | Lampeter Church of the Brethren, Lampeter, Pa. |

# Profile of Questionnaire Respondents[1]

Lengthy questionnaires were completed by 407 local church leaders. They not only responded to checklists about themselves and their churches but also provided extensive written commentary and specific examples of the kinds of changes with which their congregations had struggled. As you read the pages that follow, it's important to understand some characteristics of the individuals and churches represented in this sample.

The respondents were primarily male clergy forty years of age or older. The percentage under forty was large enough to make some comparisons possible when the data was analyzed. Those persons in lay positions were primarily employed staff members, such as Christian education directors, youth workers, and church business administrators. We did not ask for ethnic identification on the questionnaires. Comments and examples reported by respondents make it clear that some ethnic clergy serving ethnic congregations were part of the sample.

## *Age and Gender*

Age:

| | |
|---|---|
| 20-29 | 5.49% |
| 30-39 | 18.95% |

|  |  |  |
|---|---|---|
|  | 40-49 | 34.41% |
|  | 50-64 | 29.68% |
|  | 65 or older | 11.47% |
| Male: | 81.14% |  |
| Female: | 18.86% |  |
| Clergy: | 88.34% |  |
| Lay: | 11.66% |  |

## Denominational Affiliation

The largest number of respondents were United Methodists, 30.22%, followed by Presbyterians, 11.30%. Each of the other identified denominations constituted less than 10% of the respondents. A total of 5.9% were in denominations which represented less than .70% of the respondents, or did not indicate denominational affiliation.

The large number of United Methodists no doubt relates to the percentage of those on the mailing list of Net Results, through which some questionnaires were distributed, and to the fact that Steve Clapp distributed surveys at some United Methodist leadership events. Steve also had the survey completed by a large number of judicatory executives in two denominations, but we decided not to include those results in this report because of the desire to focus the results shared here on the local-church level.

| | |
|---|---|
| United Methodist | 30.22% |
| Presbyterian (USA) | 11.30% |
| Disciples | 8.60% |
| American Baptist | 6.39% |
| Reformed | 5.16% |
| Evangelical Lutheran | 5.16% |
| Church of the Brethren | 4.91% |
| Mennonite | 4.67% |
| United Church of Christ | 4.18% |
| Southern Baptist | 3.19% |
| Lutheran-Missouri Synod | 2.95% |
| Church of God | 2.70% |
| Brethren in Christ | 2.46% |
| Nazarene | 1.47% |
| Evangelical Friends | 0.74% |
| Unidentified or Other | 5.90% |

## Church and Community Size

The respondents were in churches definitely above average in size, based on average worship attendance, with 39.45% averaging more than 200 persons on Sunday morning. Slightly more than a third were in rural or small-town settings, with the rest in medium-sized, suburban, or urban settings.

### Average Worship Attendance

| | |
|---|---|
| Under 50 | 5.21% |
| 50-75 | 7.20% |
| 76-100 | 12.66% |
| 101-200 | 32.68% |
| Over 200 | 39.45% |
| Unidentified | 2.73% |

### Community Description

| | |
|---|---|
| Urban | 13.86% |
| Suburban | 33.42% |
| Medium-sized | 16.58% |
| Small Town | 26.73% |
| Rural | 8.17% |
| Unidentified | 1.24% |

## Growth or Decline Mode

When asked to identify whether their churches were growing, declining, or holding even on membership, a whopping 42.33% said their churches were in a growth mode; only 16.34% identified a decline mode.

Since the vast majority of the respondents were from mainline churches, those figures are far more positive than the norm within the denominations represented. While this could represent overly optimistic thinking by the respondents, it is also likely that the means by which the surveys were distributed resulted in responses coming heavily from churches having more positive membership experiences than the norm.

The means of distribution, through a sample of the Net Results mailing list and through leadership seminars, were chosen precisely because we were especially interested in leaders who were having positive experiences in terms of growth. We felt confident that any sample would include plenty of churches in decline. Although we requested only the subjective assessment of the respondents, rather than empirical data on growth or decline, it would appear that we were successful in reaching a substantial number of people who are not currently experiencing signficant decline in the churches they serve.

| | |
|---|---|
| Primarily in a growth mode | 42.33% |
| Holding its own | 38.86% |
| Primarily in a decline mode | 16.34% |
| Unidentified | 2.48% |

## Respondent Background

About 3/4 of the respondents have been at their current churches for three years or longer, and an impressive 26.87% have been there more than ten years. The lay persons completing the survey did not differ significantly from the clergy, in terms of years at the church. The majority of lay persons completing the survey, however, were staff members, so the tenure being similar to that of clergy is not surprising.

The average number of years at the current church was lowest for United Methodists, which is not surprising, given the fairly frequent moves that generally go along with that denomination's appointive system. Even within that denomination, an impressive 20.51% had been in the same church more than ten years.

The vast majority of the respondents had been regular in church activity as children. That information was requested on the questionnaire, in an effort to determine whether any particular attitudes correlated with church activity as a child. We did not determine any significant relationships there, but it is interesting to note that pastors who "almost never" were involved in the church as children were more likely than others to be pastoring a church with an average attendance more than 200 a Sunday, and to have a tenure of more than ten years at the church currently being served.

## Number of Years at This Church

| | |
|---|---|
| Under 1 Year | 9.20% |
| 1-2 Years | 15.92% |
| 3-5 Years | 25.37% |
| 6-10 Years | 20.40% |

|                |        |
|----------------|--------|
| Over 10 Years  | 26.87% |
| Unidentified   | 2.24%  |

## Church Involvement as a Child

|              |        |
|--------------|--------|
| Regular      | 83.17% |
| Occasional   | 8.91%  |
| Almost Never | 5.20%  |
| Unidentified | 2.72%  |

## Respondent Attitudes Toward the Church

Most respondents described their attitude toward their current local church with words like *excited, optimistic,* and *deeply committed.* A significant minority, however, were *discouraged, pessimistic, or ready to quit.*

(told to check as many as apply)

|                   |        |
|-------------------|--------|
| Excited           | 38.61% |
| Optimistic        | 54.21% |
| Deeply committed  | 66.58% |
| Discouraged       | 23.27% |
| Pessimistic       | 7.67%  |
| Ready to quit     | 4.46%  |

Almost 60% of the respondents indicated that their current church "very readily" or "somewhat readily" accepts change. The majority of those were "somewhat" rather than "very" readily, but that still seems a reasonably positive assessment for our current time.

## Church Accepts Change

|                   |        |
|-------------------|--------|
| Very Readily      | 13.12% |
| Somewhat Readily  | 45.30% |
| Reluctantly       | 36.63% |
| Rarely            | 3.71%  |
| Unidentified      | 1.24%  |

For comparison, in two groups of denominational executives with whom Steve Clapp shared the questionnaire, the overall assessment was that almost 2/3 of the churches for which they were responsible only reluctantly or rarely accepted change.

The executives could have been pessimistic and the local church pastors and staff optimistic. Since more of the churches seem to be in growth-mode than the norm, and since the average tenure of respondents is so high, however, it seems more likely that the churches represented accept change better than the average. The extensive written comments of the respondents confirm that conclusion and, in some instances, share the strategies by which congregations were helped to become more open to change.

# NOTES

## Introduction

1. John P. Kotter, *A Force for Change: How Leadership Differs from Management* (New York: The Free Press, 1990), p. 32.
2. Ibid., pp. 83-84.

## 1. The Newness of You

1. Adapted from an anonymous Andrew Center survey response.
2. Norman Shawchuck and Roger Heuser, *Leading the Congregation* (Nashville: Abingdon Press, 1993), p. 126.
3. M. Scott Peck, *The Road Less Traveled* (New York: Simon & Schuster, 1978), p. 15.
4. Max DePree, *Leadership Is an Art* (New York: Doubleday, 1989), p. 47.
5. Roy Oswald, in the flyer "Clergy Self-Care" (Washington D.C.: Alban Institute Publications, 1992).
6. Stephen Covey, *The Seven Habits of Highly Effective People* (New York: Simon & Schuster, 1989), pp. 68-70.
7. From a telephone interview with Martha D. Matteson, December 17, 1993.
8. From a telephone interview with Dick Shreckhise, January 18, 1994.
9. Covey, *Seven Habits*, p. 42.
10. Tony Campolo, *The Kingdom of God Is a Party* (Dallas: Word, 1990), pp. 39-40.
11. For further discussion of the paradigm perspective in change, see Joel Arthur Barker, *Future Edge: Discovering New Paradigms of Success* (New York: William Morrow & Co., 1992) and Doug Murren, *Leadershift* (Ventura, Calif.: Regal Books, 1994).
12. William Easum, "Ten Observations That Will Change the Way You Think," *The Easum Report*, Volume 1, Issue 1, pp. 1, 3.

13. For a more detailed analysis of future trends and their implications, see Paul Mundey, *Riding the River: Congregational Outreach and the Currents of the 21st Century* (Elgin, Ill.: Andrew Center Resources, 1994).

14. From a telephone interview with Margaret Twesme, November 22, 1993.

15. Some of the best newsletters for keeping current in the area of congregational effectiveness include:
    *The Easum Report,* William Easum, ed., 21st Century Strategies, now available from:
    *Net Results,* Herb Miller, ed., Net Results Resource Center, 5001 Ave. N, Lubbock, TX 79412-2993.
    *New Beginnings,* Paul Mundey, ed., The Andrew Center, 1451 Dundee Ave., Elgin, IL 60120.

16. Sources of workshop and seminar listings include:
    The Alban Institute, Suite 433 North, 4550 Montgomery Ave., Bethesda, MD 20814-3341.
    The Andrew Center, 1451 Dundee Ave., Elgin, IL 60120 (phone: 1-800-774-3360).
    Net Results Resource Center, 5001 Ave. N, Lubbock, TX 79412-2993.

17. Reggie McNeil is experimenting with an innovative style of clergy continuing education in the South Carolina conference of the Southern Baptist Church. He is forming learning clusters of pastors. Each cluster focuses on four core areas of curriculum: paradigm issues, leadership issues, personal issues, and resource issues. McNeil can be contacted at the South Carolina General Board, 190 Stoneridge Dr., Columbia, SC 29210-8239.

18. From a telephone interview with James Chronister, December 8, 1993.

19. Ibid.

20. Elmer Towns, *Ten of Today's Most Innovative Churches* (Ventura, Calif.: Regal Books, 1990), p. 30.

21. John Ortberg and Dallas Willard, "The Spiritually Authentic Leader" (Pasadena: Fuller Evangelistic Association, 1992), audio tape.

## 2. Lighting the Way

1. From a telephone interview with Fred Bernhard, November 22, 1993.

2. From a telephone interview with Irvin Heishman, December 16, 1993.

3. Paul Mundey, *Change and the Established Congregation* (Elgin, Ill.: The Andrew Center, 1994), p. 29.

4. Lyle E. Schaller, *Strategies for Change* (Nashville: Abingdon Press, 1993), p. 28.

5. From a telephone interview with Joe Harding, December 29, 1993.

6. Burt Nanus, *Visionary Leadership* (San Francisco: Jossey-Bass, 1992), p. 31.

7. Quoted in Tom Peters, *Thriving on Chaos* (New York: Alfred A. Knopf, 1987), p. 404.

8. From a telephone interview with Kathleen Kline Chesson, December 15, 1993.

9. George Bernard Shaw, *Saint Joan* (Baltimore: Penguin Books, 1968), p. 59.

10. From a telephone interview with Mark Miller-McLemore, December 9, 1993.

11. James S. Hewitt, ed., *Illustrations Unlimited* (Wheaton, Ill.: Tyndale, 1988), p. 210.

12. From a telephone interview with Joe Harding, November 30, 1993.

13. From a telephone interview with Dick Boyd, November 30, 1993.

14. Peter Drucker, *Innovation and Entrepreneurship* (New York: Harper Collins, 1985), pp. 139-40.

15. James A. Belasco, *Teaching the Elephant to Dance* (New York: Penguin Group, 1990), p. 124.
16. An excellent book to guide such a committee is Lyle Schaller, *Create Your Own Future!* (Nashville: Abingdon Press, 1991).
17. George Barna, *Without a Vision, the People Perish* (Glendale, Calif.: The Barna Research Group, 1991), p. 129.
18. Ron Klassen, "Reversing Church Decline," *Leadership* (Summer 1993), p. 106.
19. From a telephone interview with Dennis Burnett, December 7, 1993.
20. John R. Myers, "Living the Vision!" *Net Results* (November, 1993), pp. 17-18.
21. Frank Harrington, "Why Now a Long-Range Planning Committee?" (Atlanta: Peachtree Presbyterian Church, sermon preached, Sunday, September 12, 1993), pp. 1-2.
22. James S. Hewitt, ed., *Illustrations Unlimited* (Wheaton, Ill.: Tyndale, 1988), p. 411.

### 3. Missionary Maneuvers

1. James P. Wind, "Leading Congregations, Discovering Congregational Cultures," *Christian Century* (February 3-10, 1993), p. 106.
2. From a telephone interview with James Chronister, December 8, 1993.
3. Tex Sample, *Ministry in an Oral Culture* (Louisville: Westminster/John Knox Press, 1994), pp. 78-79.
4. Tim Rowland, "Sharpsburg Mayor Has No Regrets," *The Daily Mail*, Hagerstown, Md., November, 23, 1992.
5. C. Kirk Hadaway, "Church Growth (and Decline) in a Southern City," *Review of Religious Research*, Volume 23, p. 374.
6. From a telephone interview with Jim Frisbie, December 7, 1993.
7. Paul Mundey, *Change and the Established Congregation* (Elgin, Ill.: Andrew Center Resources, 1994), p. 19.
8. Ibid., p. 17.
9. From a telephone interview with T. Mac Hood, December 21, 1993.
10. The term "pay the rent" was first coined by James Glasse in his classic, *Putting It All Together in the Parish* (Nashville: Abingdon Press, 1973).
11. From a telephone interview with Priscilla Eppinger-Mendes, December 8, 1993.
12. Leonard Sweet, *Homiletics* (July-September 1993), p. 45.

### 4. Many Worlds, Many Systems

1. For a more complete and varied discussion of systems, see George Parsons and Speed Leas, *Understanding Your Congregation as a System* (Washington, D.C.: The Alban Institute, 1993).
2. Paul Mundey, *Change and the Established Congregation* (Elgin, Ill.: Andrew Center Resources, 1994), p. 16.
3. From a telephone interview with Jimmy Ross, January 17, 1994.
4. Mundey, *Change and the Established Congregation,* pp. 13-14.
5. From a telephone interview with Fred Bernhard, November 22, 1993.
6. Mundey, *Change and the Established Congregation,* p. 21.
7. Ibid., p. 21.
8. *Up to the Minute* (May 1995).

9. From a telephone interview with Irvin Heishman, December 16, 1993.
10. For a fuller discussion of options for mission-directed organization, see Kennon Callahan, *Effective Church Leadership* (San Francisco: Harper & Row, 1990), pp. 203-41.
11. Bradley Greenberg, ed., *The Kennedy Assassination and the American Public: Social Communication in Crisis* (Stanford, Calif.: Stanford University Press, 1965), p. 91.
12. Leonard Sweet, *Homiletics* (July-September 1993), p. 29.
13. From a telephone conversation with David Young, August, 1995.
14. *Up to the Minute* (September 1995).
15. For more information on the Myers-Briggs typology, see David Keirsey and Marilyn Bates, *Please Understand Me* (Del Mar, Calif.: Promethean, 1978).
16. James A. Christopher, "How to Embrace Change in the Introverted Church," *Congregations* (September-October 1995), p. 12.
17. Peter L. Steinke, *How Your Church Family Works* (Washington, D.C.: The Alban Institute, 1993), pp. 43-47.
18. Edwin Friedman, *Generation to Generation* (New York: Guilford Press, 1985), pp. 208-9.
19. For a fuller discussion of self-esteem issues and congregational life, see Steve Clapp, *Overcoming Barriers to Church Growth* (Elgin, Ill.: Andrew Center Resources, 1994).
20. Ezra Earl Jones, *Quest for Quality in the Church* (Nashville: Discipleship Resources, 1993), p. vi.
21. *Up to the Minute* (May 1995).
22. See Paul Diettrich, "Why Incremental Changes Won't Work," *Transformation,* Volume II, Number 2, (Spring 1995), pp. 1, 4, 7-10.
23. Leonard Sweet, *Homiletics* (April-June 1994), p. 25.

### 5. The Learning Congregation

1. Don Spatz and A. Aubrey Bodine, "There Is a Way Out," from *Look At It This Way* (Baltimore: Bodine & Associates, 1975).
2. Charles Handy, *The Age of Unreason* (Boston: Harvard Business School Press, 1990), p. 65.
3. Richard Lovelace, *Dynamics of Spiritual Life* (Downers Grove, Ill.: Inter-Varsity Press, 1979), p. 205.
4. Personal correspondence with Martin Brown, dated March 11, 1992, p. 3.
5. Personal correspondence with Richard Shreckhise, dated April 20, 1992.
6. From a telephone interview with Jim and Rinya Frisbie, December 7, 1993.
7. From a telephone interview with Irvin Heishman, December 16, 1993.
8. R. Paul Stevens and Phil Collins, *The Equipping Pastor: A Systems Approach to Congregational Leadership* (Washington, D.C.: The Alban Institute, 1993), p. 36.
9. From a telephone interview with Joe Harding, November 30, 1993.
10. For more information on the Teaching Church Network, write Paul D. Borden, Executive Director, Teaching Church Network, P.O. Box 39282, Minneapolis, MN 55439-0282.
11. As quoted in the Teaching Church Network brochure, June 1994.
12. From a telephone interview with Robert Cueni, November 17, 1993.

13. As quoted in Warren Bennis, *On Becoming a Leader* (New York: Addison-Wesley Publishing, 1989), p. 185.
14. From a school letter from the Elgin Academy from Steven B. Tobolsky, dated February 3, 1995.

## 6. Barn-Raising Believers

1. Elmer Towns, *An Inside Look at 10 of Today's Most Innovative Churches* (Ventura, Calif.: Regal Books, 1990), p. 31.
2. Quoted in John P. Kotter and James L. Heskett, *Corporate Culture and Performance* (New York: Free Press, 1992), p. 116.
3. From a telephone interview with Norman Shawchuck, December 22, 1993.
4. Ted Engstrom and Edward Dayton, *The Christian Leader's 60-Second Management Guide* (Waco: Word Books, 1984), pp. 79-80.
5. From a telephone interview with T. Mac Hood, December 21, 1993.
6. Charles Handy, *The Age of Unreason* (Boston: Harvard Business School Press, 1990), p. 13.
7. Arlin Rothauge, *Sizing Up a Congregation for New Member Ministry* (New York: Education for Mission and Ministry Office, Seabury Professional Services [no date]), p. 5.
8. Paul Mundey, *Change and the Established Congregation* (Elgin, Ill.: Andrew Center Resources, 1994), p. 31.
9. Ibid., p. 22.
10. Ibid.
11. From a telephone interview with Jim Hodge, November 17, 1993.
12. Mundey, *Change and the Established Congregation,* p. 23.
13. From a telephone interview with Harry Vein, December 13, 1993.
14. Knox Talbert, "Managing Change," seminar presented at Willow Creek Association International Conference, June 1994.
15. From a telephone interview with Dennis Burnett, December 7, 1993.
16. Mundey, *Change and the Established Congregation,* p. 36.
17. From a telephone interview with James S. Flora, April 18, 1995.

## 7. Bridging Toward Tomorrow

1. See, for example, William Bridges, *Managing Transitions: Making the Most of Change* (Reading, Mass.: Addison-Wesley Publishing Company, 1991).
2. Knox Talbert lecturing at the "Managing Change" seminar at the Willow Creek International Conference, June 11-18, 1994.
3. This material is adapted from information shared at the seminar "Orientation to Church Change Agentry and Consulting," held August 14-16, 1992, by Church Consultants Group, 3001 S. State, Suite 406, Ann Arbor, MI 48108.
4. Ibid., p. 36.
5. From a telephone interview with Jenny Jackson-Adams, January 11, 1994.
6. Everett M. Rogers, *Diffusion of Innovation* (New York: The Free Press, 1983), pp. 246-51.
7. From a telephone interview with Eric Anspaugh, December 9, 1993.
8. Charles Kraft, "Fear of Change Is Like Acting on a Shaky Stage," *Worship Leader* (October/November 1992), pp. 9-39.

9. Alvin Toffler, *Future Shock* (New York: Bantam Books, 1971), pp. 378ff.
10. Leonard Sweet, *Homiletics* (April-June 1993), p. 22.
11. Edgar H. Schein, *Organizational Psychology* (Englewood Cliffs, N.J.: Prentice Hall, 1980), pp. 244-45.
12. From the *Executive Galley Catalog,* April 1995, p. 34.

## 8. The Right Start

1. Burt Nanus, *Visionary Leadership* (San Francisco: Jossey-Bass, 1992), p. 36.
2. Thomas R. Harvey, *Checklist for Change* (LaVerne, Calif.: University of LaVerne, 1989), p. 57.
3. From a telephone interview with Jim Hodge, November 17, 1993.
4. Lyle Schaller, *Strategies for Change* (Nashville: Abingdon Press, 1993), p. 46.
5. From a telephone interview with Jim and Rinya Frisbie, December 7, 1993.
6. From a telephone interview with T. Mac Hood, December 21, 1993.
7. Leonard Sweet, *Homiletics* (October-December 1993), p. 14.
8. Kenneth Roman and James Maas, *The New How to Advertise* (New York: St. Martins Press, 1992), pp. 84-85.
9. "Church Mouse Has Returned from Vacation," *The Weekly Visitor,* Volume XXII, No. 29, Hagerstown Church of the Brethren, Hagerstown, Md.
10. From a telephone interview with Kathleen Kline Chesson, December 15, 1993.
11. *Parables,* 10 (July 1990), p. 8.

## 9. Grappling with Resistance

1. The concept of reducing rather than resisting resistance is based on social scientist Kurt Lewin's classic studies. For more detailed information, see Kurt Lewin, *Field Theory in Social Science* (New York: Harper & Row, 1951).
2. Paul Mundey, *Change and the Established Congregation* (Elgin, Ill.: Andrew Center Resources, 1994), pp. 26-27.
3. Knox Talbert, lecturing at "Managing Change" seminar, held at First Annual International Conference, Willow Creek Community Church, June 14-18, 1994.
4. From a telephone interview with Pastor Priscilla Eppinger-Mendes, December 8, 1993.
5. For more information on the Myers-Briggs Type Indicator, see David Keirsey and Marilyn Bates, *Please Understand Me* (Del Mar, Calif.: Promethean, 1978). For more information on the DISC Profile, contact the Carlson Learning Company, P.O. Box 1763, Minneapolis, MN 55440-9238.
6. The typology that follows is original, but was inspired by Bob Phillips, *The Delicate Art of Dancing with Porcupines: Learning to Appreciate the Finer Points of Others* (Ventura, Calif.: Regal Books, 1989).
7. As quoted by Michael Lewis, "Can You Teach an Old Church New Tricks?" *Leadership* (Summer 1993), p. 25.
8. From a telephone interview with Jenny Jackson-Adams, January 11, 1994.
9. Edwin Friedman, *Generation to Generation* (New York: Guilford Press, 1985), p. 208.
10. From a telephone interview with Kurt Snyder, January 24, 1994.
11. John Yates, "Complaining," *Leadership IX* (Summer 1993), p. 60.

12. Peter L. Steinke, *How Your Church Family Works* (Washington, D.C.: The Alban Institute, 1993), pp. 22-23.
13. Paul Mundey, *Change and the Established Congregation* (Elgin, Ill.: Andrew Center Resources, 1994), p. 25.
14. Warren Bennis, *On Becoming a Leader* (New York: Addison-Wesley Publishing, 1989), p. 149.

### 10. Bolstering Bold Beginnings

1. As told at the Church of the Brethren National Youth Conference, Ft. Collins, Col., August, 1944.
2. From a telephone interview with Mark Miller-McLemore, December 9, 1993.
3. From a telephone interview with Martha Matteson, December 17, 1993.
4. Price Pritchett, *Culture Shift* (Dallas: Pritchett Publishing Co., 1993), p. 11.
5. George Barna, *Today's Pastor* (Ventura, Calif.: Regal Books, 1994), p. 36.
6. Marilee Munger Schroggs, "Making a Difference: Fourth Presbyterian Church of Chicago," in James P. Wind and James W. Lewis, *American Congregations, Volume 1, Portraits of Twelve Religious Communities* (Chicago: University of Chicago Press, 1994), p. 513.
7. From *Executive Galley Catalog*, April 1995, p. 20.
8. Leonard Sweet, "Deserving Our Warning Sign," *Homiletics* (January-March 1994), p. 49.
9. For additional information on creating adequate support systems, see Roy Oswald, *Clergy Self-Care: Finding A Balance for Effective Ministry* (Washington, D.C.: Alban Institute, 1991), pp. 129-39.
10. Leonard Sweet, "Returning God's Call," *Homiletics* (January-March 1991), p. 13.
11. See Charles Handy, *The Age of Paradox* (Boston: Harvard Business School Press, 1994), pp. 49-59.
12. Inspired by Robert Raines, *To Kiss the Joy* (Waco: Word Books, 1973), pp. 9-10.

### Epilogue

1. From a telephone interview with Craig Haberman, December 6, 1993, quoting Loren Mead, *The Whole Truth About the Church in Twelve Pages.*
2. As quoted in George Barna, *Turn Around Churches* (Ventura, Calif.: Regal Books, 1993) p. 107.
3. Aubrey Malphurs, *Pouring New Wine into Old Wineskins* (Grand Rapids: Baker Book House, 1993), pp. 43-76.
4. Catherine Marshall, "Finding Peace on the Journey," *Christianity Today* (May 15, 1995), p. 36.
5. Ibid.

### Appendix: Research Methodology

1. Information in this section of the appendix is adapted from Paul Mundey, *Change and the Established Congregation* (Elgin, Ill.: The Andrew Center, 1994).